FIXING AMERICA
Breaking the Stranglehold of Corporate Rule, Big Media, and the Religious Right

JOHN BUCHANAN

Foreword by John McConnell,
founder of Earth Day

FWPC

Far West Publishing Company
Distributed by Sun Distributing
Santa Fe, N.M.

First Printing...2004

Copyright, 2004
by John Buchanan

Published by Far West Publishing Company
P.O. Box 5588
Santa Fe, New Mexico 87502-5588 U.S.A

ISBN: 0-89540-436-2

DEDICATION

To my mother

ACKNOWLEDGMENTS

The writing of this book was inspired by a number of people, both living and dead. Among the deceased inspirations were America's Founding Fathers, most notably the inimitable firebrand Thomas Paine, as well as Mohandas K. "Mahatma" Gandhi and former U.S. Presidents Abraham Lincoln and Franklin Delano Roosevelt. Among the living are former Berlin, New Hampshire, Mayor Richard P. Bosa, Philadelphia firewalker Robert "Cork" Kallen, jazz musician and political gadfly Brian Finigan, Veterans Administration public servant Terry Weldon, disabled veteran Jerry Simons, Russian iconoclast Jack Ross, and talk-radio hosts Meria Heller and Jack Blood.

Special places in my heart are reserved for Nelson Mandela and John McConnell, the 89-year-old founder of Earth Day, who made me believe in myself and a shared cause.

Special thanks to Skip Whitson and Joe Fatton of Sun Distributing and Far West Publishing for their tender loving care, and to the Kubiak family of Kennebunkport, Maine, for a place to work and a seat at the dinner table. Thanks to David Kubiak and Darcy Richardson for their encouragement and editing skills, and to Herman Graf and Ian Kleinert for their help. Special thanks to Gabriel Day, Riva Enteen, Janice Matthews, Mark Bilk, Dr. Robert Thorne, David Kelsey, Brian Bellitsos and Rae Shearn for their moral support and extraordinary assistance at a time of extreme adversity.

FIXING AMERICA
*Breaking the Stranglehold
of Corporate Rule, Big Media,
and the Religious Right*

CONTENTS

Foreword

"Faith in a Miraculous Change"

"United we stand, divided we fall" is a powerful slogan. But in the long run, it only works when it is applied to a cause that is just and fosters peaceful progress.

After a lifetime of trying to foster peace and justice on our planet, I am frustrated by the world of violence and injustice I see. At 89 years old, I feel that my life's work is in jeopardy today.

My father was a Pentecostal minister. He used to teach that when God created man, He was a God of love. That message is in great danger today. God gave us free will, but we have misused it to amass wealth and power among the few, while the many suffer. Today, under George W. Bush, the peaceful message of Jesus has been turned into a call to war in the name of God. The media are as much to blame as the President. I can never get them to give any attention to a message of peace. Instead, they promote hate, greed, fear, and lust.

That makes them more money.

The leaders in our society, which claims to be Christian, now personify a lust for power rather than love for our fellow human beings. But I continue to have faith that we will have a miraculous change of our destiny before we are past the point of no return, that we can move as a human family toward a peaceful, prosperous future for all.

Today, America reminds me of the story about a man who was walking along a path at night and saw a mud puddle. But when he focused on it he noticed the reflection of the stars. America is like an ugly mud puddle. But when we focus on the stars, it brings new hope for the future.

In trying to accent the positive, I have found that most of the world's religions teach that we should obey the Golden Rule: "Love your neighbor as yourself." Today, I'm afraid, that message is being drowned out by never-ending media coverage of hatred and needless war.

In the Age of Science, we are confronted by an amazing cosmos, an amazing planet, yet we can't get along as human beings. It seems that the source, purpose, and meaning of life are more of a mystery than ever.

All individuals and institutions have a mutual responsibility to act as trustees of Earth, seeking good choices in ecology, economics, and ethics that will eliminate pollution, poverty, and violence; foster peaceful progress; awaken the wonder of life; and realize the best potential for the future of the human adventure. In order to accomplish those goals, we need to put aside our differences and focus on the things we have in common. In order to do that, we need a shared sense of hope, a collective vision for redemption.

During my lifetime I have known 33 Nobel laureates and three Secretaries-General of the UN. None of them, in terms of courage and conviction, had anything on John Buchanan, the author of this simple, honest book. In *Fixing America*, he has demonstrated the kind of vision that can change the U.S. and the world for the better. None of the important issues he raises are being discussed by either political party during this Presidential election year.

In the final years of my life, I hope and pray that a message of peace and justice can overcome the message we now see as dominant in our public debate.

This book is a good beginning.

John McConnell
Founder of Earth Day (March 1970)
and the Minute for Peace (1963)

Introduction

"Simple Facts, Plain Arguments, and Common Sense"

In the classic 1975 film *Network*, disgruntled news anchor Howard Beale suffers an on-the-air nervous breakdown. As the result of an epiphany that has enlightened him that life in corporate-controlled America is brutal and unfair, he implores his viewers to "go to the window, stick your head out, and yell, 'I'm mad as hell and I'm not going to take it any more.'"

Across the country, outraged citizens – from little old ladies to white-collar execs – hoist their windows and scream.

Two decades earlier, a lesser-known but equally incensed American hero had made a similar speech in real life. "If the people of this nation fully understood what Congress has done to them ... they would move on Washington. They would not wait for an election." The speaker was U.S. Senator George Wilson Malone of Nevada. Nearly a half-century later, his forgotten words resonate like the rhetoric of a populist revolution.

Today, freedom and the very notion of self-rule that Thomas Jefferson and his fellow Founding Fathers envisioned more than 200 years ago are being eroded before our eyes. Meanwhile, "we the people" – the majority caught in the middle of a culture war between opposing, extremist minorities on the right and left – remain mysteriously silent, sedated by a deadly blend of material comfort and political correctness.

To the determined minority involved in political and social reforms, daily life has devolved into a matter of fighting for or against abortion, for or against gun control, for or against same-sex marriage. As if the best interests of "the greatest nation in history" could be any further subverted, such specific-issue turf battles are almost always decidedly partisan, with Republicans staking out the official GOP position, and reactionary Democrats lamely putting forth a "Democratic alternative."

But almost no one speaks any more of what is good for *all* Americans, judged not in the framework of special-interest politics, but in the spirit of the Declaration of Independence. As a result, our system of government has developed fissures that have become cracks that threaten to crumble open into crevices that will swallow the American Dream.

Given the reality that only half of us vote and that fewer than that truly comprehend any particular issue of the day, it is perhaps amazing that our experiment in freedom and democracy has survived as long as it has.

But it has survived with an alarming caveat: If there is a fatal flaw in participatory democracy, it is the *participatory* part.

In that sense, the corporate mass media have been instruments of alienation rather than inspiration. Bearing in mind that the ancient Greeks had Socrates and Plato as prominent commentators on the issues of the day, we must face the sad reality that in the age of instant global communication, we have Bill O'Reilly, Ann Coulter, and Sean Hannity, right-wing propagandists who earn millions of dollars spewing partisan, elitist poison on our public airwaves.

The ancient Greeks had, for entertainment, Euripides and Aeschylus. In the 1950s and 60s, Americans had live-TV drama from writers of the stature of Arthur Miller and Rod Serling. In 2004, we get "reality TV."

Such is the sorry grist of our "postmodern" culture mill.

Ultimately, then, we have gotten the "government" we deserve: a dysfunctional consortium of giant transnational corporations, private international bankers, million-dollar lobbyists, a corporate-controlled media, a right-wing militarist "Christian" regime that launches wars in the name of God, and bought-and-and-paid-for career politicians who have looted the U.S. Treasury and stripped us of our individual dignity and optimistic futures for our children.

Meanwhile, "we the people" – descendants of the men and women who made that battle cry a symbol for the rest of the world in 1776 and ever since – have sat by and watched, while doing almost nothing to defend that for which the United States of America supposedly stands: that "all men are created equal, with the unalienable rights of life, liberty, and the pursuit of happiness."

In 2004, that sounds more like the punch line for a perverse capitalist joke, a tag line for a Madison Avenue campaign commercial, than a basis for enduring democracy and human fulfillment.

Given the principles provided by Jefferson in the Declaration of Independence – that the power of governance must be vested in ordinary people rather than kings or lesser despots, and that citizenship in such a republic carries with it, by definition, the awesome responsibility for all national burdens and traumas - "we the people" have failed, miserably. We have abdicated our responsibilities as a free people, while becoming conversant on the social significance of the Kobe Bryant rape case, Laci Peterson murder case, or Michael Jackson child molestation case.

Until we understand and address the real nature of our problems, we have no hope of solving them. Until we force truth into the light, we are destined to reside in darkness. This book, then, is offered as a primer for political discourse, a citizen's manifesto for revolt.

"In the following pages, I offer nothing more than simple facts, plain arguments, and common sense," Thomas Paine wrote in the introduction to *Common Sense* in 1776, "and have no other preliminaries to settle with the reader, than that he will divest himself of prejudice and presupposition, and suffer his reason and his feelings to determine for themselves."

So powerful were the reason and feelings unleashed by Paine's eloquent treatise that it helped prompt the American Revolution. "*Common Sense* stated the case for freedom from England's rule with a logic and a passion that roused the public opinion of the Colonies to a white heat," Sidney Hook wrote in the introduction to *The Essential Thomas Paine* (Mentor Books, 1969). "It presented the severest indictment of hereditary monarchy and privilege that had ever been penned until that time."

Today, "we the people" live under the boot heel of a different sort of hereditary monarchy, ruled by an American dynasty of wealthy elites and global corporations, facilitated by a treasonous Congress and apathetic public.

"A long habit of not thinking a thing wrong gives it a superficial appearance of being right," Paine wrote in *Common Sense*. In 2004, that sentiment is an indictment of the American people.

"The cause of America is in a great measure the cause of all mankind," Paine observed. With a sort of daunting irony and unintended consequence as the world's only superpower in the post-Cold War world, that is more true today than in 1776, as we reach for our national destiny in challenging times.

Nothing has ever come easily in America. From the rights of women and African-Americans to vote, to the rights of workers to organize, to the rights of legal defendants to be free from abuse by prosecutors and the police, Americans have struggled, fought, and died to make their country a better place for their descendants and to set an example for the rest of the world.

Now, more than ever, in the troubled post-9/11 environment we helped to create, we must face a new test.

"The ultimate arbiter is the people of the Union," Thomas Jefferson wrote in an 1823 letter, near the end of his life. His philosophy carried with it the genetic imprint of a man who had helped overthrow a tyrannical and mighty king in order to be able to make such a preposterous and unprecedented boast.

The Merriam-Webster Dictionary defines arbiter as "a person, or agency, with power to decide a dispute."

If Jefferson and Paine were right, then it's time to go to the window and make celluloid hero Howard Beale proud.

It's time to go to the window and yell, *"I'm mad as hell and I'm not going to take it any more."*

John Buchanan
Portsmouth, New Hampshire
July 4, 2004

I

The Rise of the Corporate State

Chapter 1

Who Really Owns the U.S. Government?

W alk into any office, classroom, VFW hall, bingo parlor, or 7-Eleven store, and pose a simple question: "Who *really* owns the U.S. government, 'we the people,' or the Fortune 500?" The overwhelming majority of those present will tell you, without hesitation, that giant corporate interests control 2004 America – that you and they are, in effect, slaves to consumerism and debt, and the unbridled greed and dehumanizing competition that deadly duo have engendered.

Go a step further and ask whether "truth and honor" still matter in the "postmodern," pop-culture United States of America, and you will be greeted with a resounding "No," from across the political and demographic spectrums.

Taken together, such grim sentiments, bred of cynicism and reinforced on every front, across generations, spell disaster for the singular vision put forth in 1776 by Thomas Jefferson in the Declaration of Independence. Worse still is the fact that the average American now thinks of his or her government as *something apart* from the citizenry itself, a cancerous tumor of corporate and political tyranny metastasizing out of control.

The disquieting reality is that any honest American today, from factory worker to farmer, schoolteacher to scientist, knows the truth, at least in his or her social conscience, but is almost helpless to acknowledge it, out of deep-seated fear and frustration. Because the average American no longer has any real sense of how to remedy the ills of the country, the average American today is dysfunctional as a citizen.

Such simple yet undeniable failure is a gross betrayal of the noble, simple concept for which Thomas Jefferson, James Madison, Thomas Paine, and the rest of our Founding Fathers risked dangling at the end of a rope – that the many should not be governed by a greedy, self-interested few, that humankind has a God-given right to govern itself for the good of all.

At the dawn of the 21st century, such once-revered idealism has been abandoned to what appears to be a cold, hard reality. The rights of citizens have been relentlessly usurped and suppressed by transnational corporations motivated by nothing other than profits. The "rights" of corporations – equated to those of "persons" in a still-misinterpreted 1886 U.S. Supreme Court ruling – have been upheld and expanded by federal courts that have betrayed the very citizens they were, in principle, created to protect. The apparatus of government has been reordered from the provision of "life, liberty, and the pursuit of happiness" to enforcement of the "economic growth" and "globalization" that sustain the ever-increasing power and wealth of corporations. Meanwhile, citizens – "we the people" – have lost faith in ourselves as sovereign rulers of our own country.

In the process, Thomas Jefferson has been made to look like a liar. Everything our Founding Fathers worried about as unintentional future consequences of their courage and patriotism has come to pass.

"There must be a positive passion for the public good, the public interest, honor, power, and glory, established in the minds of the people, or there can be no ... government, nor any real liberty, and this public passion must be superior to all private passions," John Adams observed in 1776.

By that standard, America today is doomed to a destiny the average citizen can hardly imagine.

"The individual owes the exercise of all his faculties to the service of his country," John Quincy Adams wrote in 1818, an ethic of good citizenship that John F. Kennedy tried to reignite in the early 1960s with his long-since reality-withered "Ask not what your country can do for you, but what you can do for your country."

By that standard, the average American of 2004 is guilty of treason.

"Government and the people do not in America constitute distinct bodies," Thomas Paine wrote in 1782. "They are one, and their interests are the same."

By that standard, "we the people" suffer socio-political schizophrenia.

Today, we find, if we look honestly upon ourselves as a nation, that there is little positive passion for the public good, that private passions have alienated us from ourselves and our fellow human beings, that service to one's country is a sort of chore rather than a duty, and – most of all perhaps – that "we the people" have given up on our government as a source of any genuine hope for as-yet-unborn generations.

How did we end up like this? Where did we go wrong?

The simple truth is that "we the people," in return for the promise of a higher standard of living after the horrors of the Great Depression and World War II, have slowly yet steadily surrendered our genuine and enduring human interests to the greed-motivated institutional interests of ever-larger corporations, both as employees and consumers. Most important, we have surrendered our belief that "we the people" do, in fact, own the government and its bounty, in trust for our families and communities.

The ever-worsening imbalance between the artificial "rights" of corporations and the legitimate rights of citizens is nothing new in American political debate. Arguments on the topic among the Founding Fathers and their closest advisers and constituents pre-date the signing of the Constitution, based on a long history of abuses and tyranny by the business interests of the colonial powers, including England.

"Much of America's history has been shaped by a long and continuing struggle for sovereignty between people and corporations," author and economic-reform activist David C. Korten observed in his groundbreaking and enormously important 1995 book, *When Corporations Rule the World* (Kumarian Press), now in its second edition.

Although the problems of "special interests" and corporate privilege can be traced back to the earliest days of the American republic, modern manifestations – such as decimation of the environment, human rights abuses, and virtual abandonment of millions of Americans viewed as "less fortunate" – are a result of social and political developments of the past few decades.

Chapter 2

An "Unholy Alliance" of Government and Business

Over the past 30 years, three powerful forces that would each help change, for the worse, the course of America as a nation began to converge: a sudden wave of corporate mergers and acquisitions that created giant transnational corporations and ultimately the predatory phenomenon of "globalization;" a conglomerate-owned media that put "news" and "information" in ever fewer hands and turned them into ever more meaningless and malicious diversion from truth and reality; and a declining turnout of voters at the polls, born of disillusionment and cynicism at the office water cooler and family dinner table.

Beginning in the mid-1970s, in the psychic wake of the Vietnam War, the Watergate scandal, and the resignation of a U.S. President and Vice President as scoundrels, a large proportion of the U.S. population began to lose faith in the civics lessons we had learned in our youth: that "America the Beautiful" is "the greatest nation in the history of the world," that "all men are created equal," that we are a government "of the people, by the people, and for the people."

Instead, we have ended up with government of the corporation, by the corporation, for the corporation – at the expense of the best interests of "we the people" and the world.

"Perhaps the greatest threat to freedom and democracy in the world today comes from the formation of unholy alliances between government and business," billionaire international financier George Soros wrote in *Public Affairs* in 2000. "This is not a new phenomenon. It used to be called fascism ... The outward appearances of the democratic process are observed, but the powers of the state are diverted to the benefit of private interests." More than a half-century earlier, the Italian dictator Benito Mussolini had put it more succinctly: "Fascism should more appropriately be called corporatism, because it is a merger of state and corporate power."

In the wake of the Great Depression, Franklin Delano Roosevelt said: "The real truth of the matter is ... that a financial element in the large centers has owned the government of the U.S. since the days of Andrew Jackson." On another occasion, FDR noted that "the first truth is that the liberty of a democracy is not safe if the people tolerate the growth of private power to a point where it becomes stronger than their democratic state itself. That, in essence, is fascism – ownership of government by an individual, a group, or by any other controlling power. Among us today a concentration of private power without equal in history is growing."

But of all the mighty and eloquent voices raised against the rise of the corporate state, perhaps U.S. Supreme Court Justice Louis Brandeis put it most bluntly: "We can have a democratic society or we can have the concentration of great wealth in the hands of the few. We cannot have both."

Today, in the era of a ruling white corporate dynasty and the private-sector plunder of billions of taxpayer dollars by brazen institutional criminals such as Enron and Halliburton, history's stern warnings have become harsh reality. Yet, few Americans seem to notice or care.

One can only wonder what U.S. legends such as Jefferson, Paine, and FDR, whose thoughts and deeds helped forge our national heritage, would think of the pharmaceutical industry, which fleeces the populace for life-saving drugs, or Halliburton, which is paid billions of dollars to support a fraudulent war in Iraq, only to be caught red-handed stealing from U.S. taxpayers and abusing the trust of U.S. troops. Under the onslaught of such treachery, "we the people" do little to stop our fiscal and psychological rape at the hands of artificial entities called corporations, which are supposedly accountable to a "public" charter in the first place.

The sad truth is, however, that it is neither fair nor reasonable to blame drug companies or war profiteers for stealing. It is *our fault* because "we the people" let them get away with it. Even worse, it is not as if we don't know that our country has been hijacked, stolen from us by faceless, middle-aged, white, wealthy male "titans of industry" who have but a single goal – the sole purpose of capitalism – the creation of more capital. In *When Corporations Rule the World*, David C. Korten wrote: "The powerful have consolidated the nation's wealth into their own hands and absolved themselves of the responsibility for their less fortunate neighbors."

Before the collapse of the Soviet Union, humankind worried about its ultimate destruction by nuclear weapons. Today, a much more realistic worry is our demise through the Armageddon of corporatism's unmitigated global greed, exacerbated by the ignorance and apathy of those they oppress.

Chapter 3

A Monolith of
"Unprecedented Negative Proportions"

I f any positive change is to be accomplished before it is too late, it must be understood that there is no moral, ethical, or ideological component to capitalism other than profit and the progeny of more capital. That is, in fact, its inherent and fatal flaw, the root cause of its long and worsening abuses of the self-interests of human beings. The only purpose to corporations of "we the people" of the U.S., or the people of any nation, is to be affordable "labor" or willing, voracious "consumer." Preferably, we will be both, in debt until the day we die in a new equivalent of indentured servitude.

It is equally important to understand that there is an ample empirical record to support the premise that 21st century corporate capitalism, as perpetrated by the Fortune 500 with the duplicity of the U.S. government, is among the most destructive evils in the history of mankind.

Even Adam Smith, who published *The Wealth of Nations*, the Bible of modern economics, in the same fateful year

Thomas Jefferson penned the Declaration of Independence, warned of the dangers of capitalism run amok. "It is ironic that corporate libertarians regularly pay homage to Adam Smith as their intellectual patron saint," David C. Korten wrote in *When Corporations Rule the World*, "since it is obvious to even the most casual reader of his epic work ... that Smith would have vigorously opposed most of their claims and policy positions. For example, corporate libertarians fervently oppose any restraint on corporate size or power. Smith, on the other hand, opposed any form of economic concentration on the ground that it distorts the market's natural ability to establish a price that provides a fair return on land, labor, and capital; to produce a satisfactory outcome for both buyers and sellers; and to optimally allocate society's resources.

"Through trade agreements, corporate libertarians press governments to provide absolute protection for the intellectual property rights of corporations," Korten continued. "Smith was strongly opposed to trade secrets as contrary to market principles, and would have vigorously opposed governments enforcing a person or corporations' claim to the right to monopolize a lifesaving drug or device and to charge whatever the market would bear."

In addition, Korten noted in the most recent edition of his heroic book, it has been established rather clearly that even the rank-and-file of corporate America are aware of what is happening. In September 2000, *Business Week* "released survey results that found 72 percent of Americans believe corporations have too much power over too many aspects of American life," Korten reported. "Seventy-three percent feel top executives of U.S. companies are overpaid ... Ninety-five percent believe corporations should sacrifice some profit for the sake of making things better for their workers and communities."

"A related editorial," Korten wrote, "made four recommendations to *Business Week*'s corporate readers that could be copied right off protestor banners: First, get out of politics ... then take responsibility for overseas factories, spread the wealth, and pay attention to social issues."

Unfortunately, however, actions speak louder than words, and the momentarily self-aware readers of *Business Week* have failed to act on such sentiments. In the meantime, "we the people" have continued to buy the myth that unchecked corporate growth and the higher standard of living it promotes are good for us under the banner of "economic growth."

"People who celebrate technology say it has brought us an improved standard of living, which means greater choice, greater leisure, and greater luxury," wrote Jerry Mander, another economic reformer, in his 1991 book, *In the Absence of the Sacred: The Failure of Technology and the Survival of the Indian Nations* (Sierra Club Books). "None of these benefits informs us about human satisfaction, happiness, security, or the ability to sustain life on earth." In fact, Mander declared, "technological evolution is leading to something new: a worldwide, interlocked, monolithic, technical-political web of unprecedented negative proportions."

It is not as if the average American does not understand what is happening. "A [1991] Kettering Foundation report captured the mood of the American electorate," Korten noted in his book. "Americans describe the present political system as impervious to public direction, a system run by a professional political class and controlled by money, not votes." In philosophical concurrence with Mander's declaration of a negative monolith, Korten wrote, "the things that most of us really want – a secure means of livelihood, a decent place to live, healthy and uncontaminated food to eat, good education and health care for our children, a clean and vital natural environment – seem to slip further from the grasp of most of the world's people with each passing day ... We find a profound and growing suspicion among thoughtful people the world over that something has gone very wrong. ... Approximately 1.2 billion of the world's people struggle desperately to live on less than $1 a day … Nearly a billion people go to bed hungry each night."

As human beings and citizens of "the greatest nation in the history of the world," is that a legacy "we the people" want to leave in our names?

Chapter 4

Uncivil War:
Corporate Culture vs. Human Culture

"A culture is a collection of shared beliefs about how things are," acclaimed author and radio talk show host Thom Hartmann wrote in the introduction to his 2002 book, *Unequal Protection: The Rise of Corporate Dominance and the Theft of Human Rights* (Rodale). "These beliefs are associated with myths and histories that form a self-reinforcing loop, and the collection of these beliefs and histories form the stories that define a culture. Usually unnoticed, like the air we breathe, these stories are rarely questioned. Yet their impact can be enormous."

As painful yet inspirational historic examples, Hartmann, a Vermont-based former international relief worker, cites the permissibility of slave ownership and the exclusion of women from the political process, both of which were eventually corrected by the force of human spirit and grass-roots activism.

Today, much of such grass-roots social activism, Hartmann noted with optimism, is based on a simple but daunting challenge: ending the reign of giant transnational corporations and their partners in American politics as the driving forces behind life in the 21st century. Hartmann's premise for revolution is essentially based on a single, simple principle: ending the myth, enacted by the U.S. Supreme Court in 1886, that corporations have the rights of persons. In that little-known ruling, *Santa Clara County v. Southern Pacific Railroad*, the court granted the rights of free speech and other civil liberties, as outlined in the Bill of Rights, to the artificial and publicly chartered institutions known as corporations since the 16th century.

With the obvious exception of its selection of George W. Bush as President of the United States in December 2000, no Supreme Court ruling has done more damage to the self-interest of the American people. In one of history's most astonishing judicial ironies, the court relied on the Fourteenth Amendment, intended to protect the rights of freed slaves after the Civil War, as its justification for what has become known as the doctrine of "corporate personhood." In a ruling deviously devoid of comment, the court bestowed on corporations – until then artificial entities created under the public trust by governments – the same rights to influence government and redress grievances as those bestowed on citizens. The decision paved the way "for corporations to use their wealth to dominate public thought and discourse," noted another journalist, Anup Shah, in a December 2002 article entitled "The Rise of Corporations," posted at *Globalissues.org*.

By the end of the 19th century, journalist Jeffrey Kaplan wrote in *Orion* magazine (November-December 2003), "states had largely eliminated restrictions on corporations owning each other, and by 1904, 318 corporations owned 40 percent of all manufacturing assets ... Throughout the 20th century, federal courts have granted U.S. corporations additional rights that once applied only to human beings – including those of 'due process' and 'equal protection.' Corporations, in turn, have used those rights to thwart democratic efforts to check their growth and influence."

By definition, such "equality" for corporations cedes them an unfair advantage over people, for two reasons – money and manpower.

Whereas the average citizen is limited to spending his or her hard-earned money on activism, or the relatively small amount of time that can be invested, corporations can invest millions of dollars and vast staff resources – usually supplemented by Madison Avenue ad agencies and high-powered public relations firms – to get their message out, in direct contravention of the interests of the people as a whole. The battle is as much of a mismatch as Mike Tyson, in his ferocious prime, fighting a schoolboy.

As a result, economic reformers and authors Richard L. Grossman and Frank T. Adams observed more than a decade ago, "Corporations have won more rights under law than people have – rights which government has protected with armed force."

Chapter 5:

The World Trade Organization: Consent of the Governed?

Of the numerous forces that have aided and abetted giant U.S. corporate interests to the detriment of their employees and communities, none is more sinister than the World Trade Organization (WTO). If "we the people" are ever to come to terms with reality, we must understand the influence of the WTO and the tenacity with which corporate America and the U.S. government defend it.

Established on January 1, 1995, and headquartered in Geneva, Switzerland – "50 years after it was envisioned by corporate leaders and rejected by the world's nations," economic-environmental activist and researcher George Draffan noted in yet another important but little-known book, *The Elite Consensus* (Apex Press, 2003) – the WTO marked a turning point in international trade. As of May 2004, the WTO included 147 member nations, but its deceptively quiet power has more and more been dominated by the United States and its biggest G-8 competitors, the world's major economic players.

"Ironically, the WTO is among the most democratic of the multilateral organizations," *The Christian Science Monitor* reported in September 2003. "It operates on the basis of one country, one vote, and – unlike the United Nations – no member has the right to a veto. In practice, however, the U.S., Japan, and the advanced nations of Europe tend to control the agenda and overpower developing nations with skilled trade experts and superior negotiating tactics. While Brazil and China have cultivated expertise of their own, many other developing countries are too poor to afford effective representation at the WTO."

What nation's global corporations have benefited more than any other from such unfairness? The United States.

However, that is not the real problem. If the WTO were widely presumed to be a trade-oriented body whose policies and decisions ultimately secured the self-interests of human beings, such a U.S. imbalance could be hailed with national pride. But no presumption could be further from the truth.

In its article, *The Christian Science Monitor* offered a specific example of pro-U.S. WTO abuse of developing nations. "African cotton growers had a specific complaint," reporter Patrick Smith noted. "The U.S. now spends $3.6 billion annually on cotton subsidies; with almost a third of U.S. cotton production exported, American farmers claim about 40 percent of the global market. Because they are so heavily subsidized, they also depress world prices by about a quarter."

Even in the face of such inequitable facts, however, the real threats from the WTO run much deeper.

"The surface language of the WTO is about the free trade of goods and services across national borders," Richard L. Grossman and a team of researchers wrote in a pamphlet, *The WTO, the U.S. Constitution & Self-Government*, supporting the anti-WTO protests in Seattle in late 1999. "But the coercive power of the WTO is directed to limiting the authority of the majority in every country to govern – that is, to control their own labor, spend their natural wealth, use their property, conserve their resources, structure their communities, define their institutions, choose their technologies. Backed by the military power of governments, especially by the United States, the WTO is about enabling a few to rule over multitudes."

Such de facto rule by ever more powerful U.S. corporations, via decisions and directives of the WTO during its first decade of existence, has taken a heavy toll against the best interests of "we the people." "The WTO has ruled against every environmental law it has reviewed, and its decisions have resulted in weakening of the environmental and health and safety standards of several nations," Draffan established in *The Elite Consensus*. "The WTO ruled that the U.S. Clean Air Act violates trade rules; in response, the U.S. EPA weakened its regulations limiting gasoline contaminants. The WTO ruled against the U.S. Endangered Species Act provisions requiring shrimp sold in the U.S. to be caught with devices that protect sea turtles." The judicial-regulatory body also "struck down a Massachusetts law rejecting purchases from corporations doing business with the military regime in Burma," Draffan explained. "WTO trade rules forbid the consideration of non-commercial factors such as human rights in government purchasing decisions; in some cases, even a threat to bring a case before the WTO results in the gutting of laws protecting human rights, health, and safety."

Nevertheless, Draffan noted, WTO threats can be rather effective. "The U.S. weakened its dolphin-safe tuna regulations when Mexico threatened to sue," the author reported. More recently, the U.S. and European Union have threatened to pursue action before the WTO if new fuel efficiency standards for motor vehicles are legislated by sovereign nations who support environmental responsibility.

How is such destructive influence even possible?

"The WTO's ... authority stems from its ability to strike down the domestic laws, programs, and policies of its member nations and to compel them to establish new laws that conform to WTO rules," economic- reform activist and author Jerry Mander and his colleague Debi Barker wrote in a 1999 report, *Does Globalization Help the Poor?*, prepared on behalf of the International Forum on Globalization (IFOG), of which Mander, a former ad agency CEO and Sierra Club organizer, is president. "This authority extends beyond the national government level, all the way to provinces, states, counties, and cities."

And all the while, the WTO and its co-conspirators in transnational corporations and major world governments, including the U.S., sell the false notion that the WTO represents fairness and free trade.

Challenge that notion on any large scale and the result is the state-sponsored police brutality and mass media demonizing unleashed against anti-WTO protesters in Seattle in November 1999 and anti-Free Trade Area of the Americas (FTAA) opponents in Miami in late 2003.

Meanwhile, "despite their enormous ramifications, most international trade agreements remain a mystery to the average American," Jeffrey Kaplan wrote in his *Orion* article, "Consent of the Governed."

At the same time, any real concept of "free trade" and attendant worldwide human well-being, exported by the U.S. as a legacy of our Founding Fathers and subsequent victory 200 years later in the Cold War, remains a victim of corporate propaganda and lies financed with billions of dollars worth of false advertising and fraudulent public relations.

Chapter 6

21st Century "Consumerism" as Capitalist Tool

I f "we the people" are to take back our country and ensure the futures of our children and the people of the developing world, we must first understand a few simple facts about our present state of affairs. One of the most important is the difference between a 21st century "capitalist economy" – a predatory and destructive force, as exemplified by Wal-Mart and Microsoft – and a true "market economy," as defined by Adam Smith.

"The institutions of a capitalist economy are designed to concentrate control of the means of production in the hands of the few to the exclusion of the many," David C. Korten explained in *When Corporations Rule the World*. "A capitalist economy is characterized by concentrations of monopoly power, financial speculation, absentee ownership, deregulation, public subsidies, the externalization of costs, and central economic planning by mega-corporations. By contrast…a market economy, as envisioned by Adam Smith and described by market theory, [is] intended to facilitate the self-organizing process by which people engage in the production and exchange of goods and services to create adequate and satisfying livelihoods for themselves and their families. A true market economy features human-scale enterprises, honest money, rooted local ownership, and a framework of democratically chosen rules intended to maintain the conditions of efficient market function – including equity and cost internalization. It is a natural companion to democracy and a pluralistic society."

In other words, a capitalist economy benefits investors, speculators, and multi-millionaire CEOs, while a market economy benefits human beings and communities.

Which would you rather have?

In addition, "modern" markets have been transmuted by yet another reality. As humankind made its long, slow transition from caves to condominiums, our march to "prosperity" has altered the very nature of commerce conducted of "necessity." When early man bartered pelts for warm clothing in return for something of equal value and practical use, the notion was born, and lasted into the 20th century, that the science of marketing must always be based on "need." But in the post-World War II era, as America evolved into both military and economic superpower, the greed-based idea was born that markets must be "created" in order for the U.S. and world economies to grow. Hence, through the modern "science" of advertising, the "consumer" was born: a human being whose responsibility is to buy and consume goods and services he or she no longer genuinely needs, but instead *wants* – only because a false sense of "need" has been artificially created.

It is no longer enough, says the myth of a consumer culture, for "upwardly mobile" Americans to build or buy a house. We are now convinced that "living well" means having a second home, or a beach house, or a condo along a golf course. It is no longer enough to buy an automobile for transportation. We are convinced we should have a fast sports car for the weekends, a recreational vehicle for summer outings. As a result, the ethic of American "consumption" has far surpassed basic human needs and led to the ongoing depletion of planetary resources required to manufacture ever-increasing amounts of "consumer goods."

And "we the people," ignorant of the real consequences of our addiction to consumption, merrily go along with the game, to the detriment of our communities, our country, and the world. Such has been the genesis of a nation, and a world, of "haves" and "have-nots."

Chapter 7

Corporate Muscle:
A 6-Point Plan for Domination

O f the 100 largest economies in the world, 51 are corporations and only 49 are countries, based on a comparison of company sales to national gross domestic product (GDP), according to the Institute for Policy Studies (IPS), in a November 2000 report entitled *Top 200: The Rise of Corporate Global Power*. The combined sales revenues of the top 200 corporations are bigger than the combined economies of all countries on earth except the Big 10, according to the startling report. Those revenues are 18 times the combined annual income of the 1.2 billion people – 24 percent of the world's population – who live in severe poverty. Although the revenues of the top 200 are equal to 27.5 percent of total world economic activity, the companies employ only 0.78 percent of the world's workforce. Between 1993 and 1999, profits of the top 200 grew 362.4 percent, while the number of people they employ grew by only 14.4 percent.

Incredibly, according to the IPS analysis, "a full 5 percent of the top 200's combined workforce" – more than 1.14

million people – are employed by Wal-Mart, "a company notorious for union-busting and widespread use of part-time workers to avoid paying benefits."

In *The Elite Consensus*, George Draffan concluded that "...governments have become 'mere salesmen' promoting multinational corporations, which are the 'muscle and brains' of the global economy." Draffan also explained that "the flow of power to corporations is promoted by mechanisms such as corporate personhood, limits to liability, pollution permitting, and political campaign financing, and by international structures such as regulatory agencies, export credit agencies, and police forces and armies. Together, these mechanisms and structures maintain networks of tightly-held power." Corporate power is maintained via a well-defined agenda that includes a half-dozen key goals, according to Richard L. Grossman and Ward Morehouse, who co-wrote the foreword to *The Elite Consensus*.

First, corporations aim to "privatize profits." That means getting subsidies and concessions from labor and the public, lobbying for tax breaks and credits, and privatizing public resources and governmental services. Second is the "externalization of costs," which includes underpaying employees or using child labor in other countries, resisting waste recycling or cleanup up of toxic damage to the environment, and minimizing legal liabilities. If such liability is exposed, Grossman and Morehouse noted, the goal is to "sue your insurance companies to make them pay."

The third objective is to "control information." This includes the acquisition or domination through influence as major advertisers of virtually the entire U.S. media, and making "information about corporate operations and government decision-making difficult to obtain." The fourth goal is to "centralize political authority." This includes paying off injured employees or forcing legal liability cases out of local and state courts and into federal courts, and using the influence of the WTO to circumvent the protections that are left for the public within the U.S. court system.

The fifth objective is to "centralize economic authority," which means the acquisition or destruction of small or local business and all potential competition – a strategy for which Wal-Mart and Starbucks have become the exemplars. It also means having "a handful of corporations dominate every industry," in violation of traditional anti-trust regulations, and having each industry's dominant players "control the allocation of resources and the means and ends of production," as well as prices. Most destructive to local communities, perhaps, is the goal of extracting profits and sheltering them in offshore banks to escape taxes and legal liability.

Finally, Grossman and Morehouse explained, the corporate agenda calls for the removal of all barriers to trade, "regardless of whether they protect desirable industries, health and safety, human rights, or the environment." In addition, corporations seek to "make private property and the pursuit of profit the basis of all law and all social and economic policy."

In order to succeed at that goal, deep-pocketed corporations and their allies in government have quietly agreed on the role of a middleman: the ever more powerful business lobbyist, who has replaced the dedicated activist-citizen of generations past as the model for political progress.

II

*The Corporate Lobbyist as
Instrument of Subversion*

Chapter 8

An Army of Million-Dollar Enablers

One of the most serious problems facing the American people is the undue influence of corporate lobbyists. Unfortunately, however, the average American has no idea just how serious the problem actually is.

In 2002, according to a report from Political Money Line in Washington, D.C., more than 25,000 lobbyists invested $1.6 billion to get their way with Congresspersons and U.S. Senators, on everything from weaponry and pharmaceuticals to commercial farm subsidies and energy. That amounts to 48 lobbyists and $3 million for every member of Congress. "With 4,269 bills and resolutions introduced and 241 public laws enacted [in 2002]," noted the Center for Public Integrity (CPI) in Washington, in a May 2003 report entitled *Hired Guns*, "the power lobbyists have in helping to interpret – and thereby enact – legislation cannot be overestimated."

Today, the situation is even worse. Corporate lobbyists actually write much of the legislation that is rubber-stamped by Congress in your name, without proper media coverage or public debate. Meanwhile, the typical citizen, uninformed or misinformed on the issues, increasingly stressed by mere survival, has absolutely no chance of competing with the day-to-day, year-round onslaught of professional lobbyists with a single goal and relentless focus: placing the interests of their corporate patrons above the interests of the American people.

On a state and local level, "lobbyists and their employers in 39 states spent more than $715 million wining, dining, and generally influencing state lawmakers in 2002," CPI reported. "Many details about how those dollars were spent remain hidden from public view."

Is that good for "we the people," our families, our communities?

Of course it isn't. In our hearts, we know that. We just don't know what can be done about it, and therefore we accept things as they are.

"The general lack of scrutiny comes at a time when many states are struggling with their worst fiscal crises since World War II and vested interests are expending more energy to protect their turf in the marbled halls of capitols across the country," CPI concluded. "More than 34,000 of those interests – companies, issue organizations, labor unions, and others – hired a whopping 42,000 individuals to do just that, averaging almost six lobbyists – and almost $130,000 – per [state] legislator."

At issue is the basic question of relative balance of power, and the ability of "we the people" to get laws passed that benefit us and our communities rather than corporations.

"Citizens have a right to know how much lobbyists are spending to influence governmental decisions, and who the lobbyists are, and what interests they represent," Bob Stern of the Center for Governmental Studies in California told CPI. "If states don't have good disclosure for lobbying, the citizens are really missing out on very important information when looking at their state government."

In the spirit of discovering just how bad things are, CPI undertook a study of lobbyist disclosure regulations in states across the U.S. What they found should be disturbing to anyone who values the notion of open government and fairness in policymaking.

"More than half the states received a failing grade for their registration and spending disclosure requirements filed by legislative lobbyists," CPI said. "In fact, no state received an 'A' on the Center's 48-question survey."

Much of the nearly $2.3 billion paid to lobbyists in 2002 went into their own pockets as salaries. Since it is illegal for lobbyists to pay legislators for their votes, the lobbyists themselves are paid directly, often in proportion to how well they do at influencing the most critical issues on behalf of their wealthiest corporate clients. For Washington's most successful lobbyists, incomes of as much as a million dollars a year, and more, are not uncommon. In fact, as a social class, many lobbyists rank within the ruling elite one-third of one percent of the population, based on annual income.

Meanwhile, "we the people" lack the wherewithal to travel to Washington or our state capitols to lobby as mere citizens on the most vital issues facing our communities, such as education and health care. The huge salaries professional lobbyists earn, squared against our inability to do anything but be angry, mean that the deck is stacked even further against the interests of the common citizen, because the big-dollar action is conducted in the arena of the most contentious issues, where corporations face the greatest risk of infringements upon their profit margins and legal liabilities.

In addition, there are almost absurd contradictions in the laws related to the regulation of lobbying activities. As an example, a number of states forbid lobbyists to buy a legislator a cup of coffee or lunch, but allow him or her to raise thousands of dollars for an election or re-election campaign. As every American knows, elected officials are addicted to campaign cash like junkies to heroin – and the relative extent of their stupefaction is about the same, too.

Moreover, although a number of states ban giving "anything of value" to a lobbyist, they do not really define what "anything of value" is – and they still allow campaign contributions, as a total of 48 states do, according to CPI.

One example the public policy watchdog points out is the state of Wisconsin, which has a "gift ban." But Mike McCabe of the Wisconsin Ethics Board told CPI that "the gift ban … has a gaping hole in it." The reason McCabe is concerned is that he feels Wisconsin has a long and admirable history of "squeaky clean politics that has been undermined significantly by the rising costs of campaigns and their dependence on large corporate contributions," according to the CPI analysis. "The lack of willingness to adapt to changing circumstances and our inability to deal with political ethics in our state is a real problem," McCabe said.

The good news out of Wisconsin is that the state, like some others, forbids lobbyists to provide lodging, transportation, food or meals, beverages, money, or any other thing of "pecuniary" value – meaning "consisting of or given or exacted in money." The bad news out of many other states is that such pecuniary transactions constitute the majority of what is reported by lobbyists in states that don't have such a regulatory provision.

What has been the end result of all the regulatory wrangling over the years?

Just as they win on Capitol Hill in Washington and in statehouses across America, lobbyists win when it comes to regulation of their activities, because, just as it is with most other issues of the day, "we the people" don't really know what's going on and, based on our silence and inaction, we don't seem to care.

That sort of *non*-activism on the part of "common citizens" gives rich, influential lobbyists a free pass. Once again, however, it isn't fair to blame them. In today's world, an elementary school student can figure out that professional corporate lobbyists are among the most insidiously influential creatures in the political food chain. It's *our* fault – "we the people," who don't take an hour a year to do anything about the problem, but spend an hour a week watching Donald

Trump make a "final decision" about who will be his "apprentice," in a contrived corporate morality play that generates more viewers than the nightly news on the same TV network.

Meanwhile, the gravy train that enriches paid lobbyists and undermines good public policy is among the best-kept secrets and most ignored problems in Washington and across the country. Like war profiteers and billionaire media barons, big-buck lobbyists are a sort of secret society, unchallenged by "we the people."

Chapter 9

Abuse of Power as Performance Art

D isclosure laws for lobbyists and their incomes are bad enough. Their actual activities in the halls of government, however, the conflict of interests and betrayal of public trust they inflict on the citizenry, are even more insidious.

The Center for Public Integrity has reported extensively for years on the abuses of lobbyists and legislators. In one case, a Maryland legislator failed to disclose thousands of dollars in fees generated by contracts with companies seeking to do business with the state. In Massachusetts, a lobbyist whose family owned a trucking business stalled legislation that would have imposed new inspection standards on trucking companies. In Arkansas, dog-racing operators paid a state legislator to push new legislation that increased their profits. In New Mexico, a liquor merchant who also happened to be a state legislator voted against legislation that would have killed drive-up liquor outlets. In Connecticut, a legislator fought to pass legislation to build a new stadium for the New England Patriots while his law firm was retained by a company involved in the deal. The list of abuses – de facto embezzlement of public funds and institutional extortion, among others – is endless. The only reason why the activities of crooked legislators come to light more often than those of their lobbyist cronies and campaign financiers is that elected officials are watched more closely.

"Read any newspaper for a week," CPI concluded, "and you're likely to see a variation on the same theme: the story of a state legislator who's abusing his or her position of public trust for private gain." It is, in fact, easy.

In North Dakota, for example, according to CPI, legislators do not have to disclose their primary source of income. In New Jersey, they don't have to report any of their real property interests unless they're in jurisdictions where there is casino gambling. In New Hampshire, they don't have to reveal income or stock holdings. In South Carolina, they don't have to disclose any of their investments unless they own more than five percent of a company's outstanding shares and those holdings are worth more than $100,000. Perhaps the most egregious example is in Louisiana, where the income disclosure requirements are so narrowly defined that 29 of the state's 38 state senators reported *no income at all* in 1998.

In another measurement of how abused the system can be, CPI looked at the ways in which state lawmakers have stacked the deck in their own favor by trying "to render the laws meaningless by erecting formidable, and sometimes impassable, obstacle courses in front of their financial disclosure statements." Again, a few examples cited by CPI tell the story: In seven states, anyone who wants to see disclosure statements from state legislators first must *make* disclosures about their own lives. In seven states, lawmakers can, in effect, withhold disclosure information because there are no penalties for filing late reports. In six states, lawmakers have exempted themselves from disclosure requirements to ethics agencies altogether. In Hawaii, legislators excused themselves from the strictest provisions of a conflict of interests statute for state employees by defining such individuals as "any state employee *other than* state legislators" [emphasis added].

In North Dakota, a citizen who wants to see financial disclosure reports from a state legislator has to contact 53 separate county offices in which they are held. In Maryland, Montana, and North Carolina, anyone who wants to review such public records must do so in person, meaning they have to travel hundreds of miles to get to the one office in the state where they can satisfy their curiosity.

But those are generalized examples. Let's get specific to understand just how bad things have become in the "sacred" halls of government. Because so many states make it so easy for their legislators to become thieves, the abuses of elected officials, when put in context, make crooked lobbyists look like Boy Scouts.

In Ohio, according to CPI, a state senator named Roy Ray hid the fact that he was being paid $10,000 a month by Ohio Edison, one of the state's primary public utilities, while voting on bills for or against which the company had lobbied. In Florida, historically one of the most corrupt states in the country, long before the 2000 election, a state senator named Alberto Gutman took in a half-million dollars from a health care company while serving as vice chairman of the state senate's Health Care Committee. "I don't see it as a conflict," Gutman told the Fort Lauderdale-based *Sun-Sentinel* newspaper. "I try to keep my state job separate from my personal business." In Indiana, a state representative named Sam Turpin raked in a cool $50,000 from an engineering firm that did business with riverboat casinos while he sat as chairman of the Ways and Means Committee. "During the years he was paid by the company," CPI reported, "he voted on legislation that the company wanted. He was ultimately indicted for bribery, perjury, and filing a fraudulent campaign report."

There are even worse examples, especially if you believe children are important to society. In Arizona, according to the CPI report, state representative Bob Burns "pushed for legislation ... that would have made it harder to sue child-care centers ... by narrowing the definition of child abuse, requiring a higher standard of proof, and allowing such centers to purge complaints from their files in just 60 days."

Burns and his wife owned a day-care center in Arizona.

Chapter 10

The "Two-Party" System as Cash Cow

On the federal level, professional lobbyists are even more craven and out of control. "Early Wins Embolden Lobbyists for Business," blared a headline in the *Washington Post* just two months after President George W. Bush took office in January 2001. "Buoyed by their headiest week in recent memory, " wrote reporters Dan Morgan and Kathleen Day, "...lobbyists are dusting off dozens of long-stalled legislative proposals in hopes of cashing in on a new pro-business climate fostered by Republican control of the White House."

The article reported that Congress had already abolished "workplace safety rules that had been 10 years in the making" and taken up a bankruptcy reform bill that benefited creditors against citizens. The Congress "also looked ahead to a broader agenda that would pare back environmental and land-use regulations, limit corporate liability for faulty products, rewrite rules protecting the privacy of patients' medical records, cut red tape blocking new oil refineries and pipelines, and open the Arctic National Wildlife Refuge in Alaska to oil drilling."

On March 25, 2001, the *Los Angeles Times* ran a similar story, headlined "With Bush, Happy Days Are Here Again for Corporate Lobbyists." The lead paragraph, by reporters Edmund Sanders and Richard Simon, was even more to the point, perhaps: "During eight years of the Clinton administration," the Times noted, "...lobbyist Dan Danner was invited to the White House once. In two months under President Bush, he has visited seven times, three of them for events attended by the President." Danner, who represented the National Federation of Independent Business, spoke with obvious glee when he said, "We'd forgotten what it's like to have a business-friendly President in the White House. I think people underestimated George W. Bush. Things are happening more quickly than even people in the business community expected."

By his very statement, Danner differentiated "the business community" from the citizenry on whose behalf Presidents are supposedly elected in the first place. An anonymous source noted in the story that "the whole issue of whether big business is dominating this administration is extremely touchy."

If, as historians and political analysts say, a President's term is largely defined by his "first 100 days," how's that for George W. Bush's first 60?

Nearly four years later, after the ongoing debacle of millions of dollars of overcharges by Halliburton in Iraq, attempts by Boeing to defraud the Defense Department, and indicted Bush-buddy Ken Lay's rape of Enron and thousands of its innocent employees, can there be any honest doubt about which side Bush has taken in the worsening conflict between corporations and citizens?

As for the overnight rave reviews Bush got from lobbyists, perhaps Dirk Van Dongen, president of the National Association of Wholesaler-Distributors, put it best to the *Post*: "Whereas for the past eight years [under Clinton], the wind has been in our face for things of priority to the business community, it has now shifted to our backs." If nothing else, you have to give the guy credit for telling it like it is on the record. Pride of achievement is a staple of human nature, right alongside greed. We all like to crow about a win, too.

In fairness to much-demonized Republicans, it hasn't been just GOP members of Congress who have sided with big business over their constituents for decades. Both major political parties have prostituted themselves to special interests.

In fairness to George W. Bush, he is not the only 2004 Presidential candidate to have sold his soul to corporate interests. "Senator John F. Kerry, who has made a fight against corporate special interests a centerpiece of his front-running campaign for the Democratic Presidential nomination, has raised more money from paid lobbyists than any other senator over the past 15 years," the *Washington Post* reported last January. Like Bush, the *Post* noted, Kerry has used corporate lobbyists to "bundle" contributions from smaller donors into big donations of $50,000 or even more, according to the senator's own campaign reports on file with the U.S. Federal Election Commission.

A spokesman for the long-defunct Howard Dean campaign nailed Kerry even harder. "[He] has been withdrawing money from the special-interest bank for his entire career," Jay Carson told the *Post*. "Now, because it's the popular thing to do, he wants us to believe that he's going to close the account and go after the people that have funded his political career." The knockout punch on the issue was delivered by the highly respected Charles Lewis, head of the Center for Public Integrity (CPI) in Washington: "The note of reality is he has been brought to you by special interests. It is very hard for Kerry to utter this rhetoric without some hollowness to it."

In fairness to *all* politicians, the real problem is that no one can get elected to public office any more without being a policy whore to corporations and a traitor to the human constituency they allegedly represent. As long as money, and not ideas and genuine integrity, drives U.S. politics, lobbyists will drive politicians. Anyone who claims otherwise is naïve, at best.

In the specific context of "special interest politics" and the shameless, lucrative service of corporations, the "two-party system" has become a myth. With equal glee and greed, both parties have helped tip the balance of power further in the direction of corporate interests. "Congress took a first big step toward undoing the Clinton record when it scuttled a stringent Clinton administration regulation requiring business to take steps to limit repetitive-stress injuries on the job," reported the *Post*. The paper also noted that "half a dozen Democrats provided the margin of victory for repeal of the Clinton workplace rules in the Senate ... and Democratic Party organizations received donations from some of the leading groups opposing the rules."

In addition, according to the March 2001 *Los Angeles Times* story, the Bush administration had already ended "costly ergonomic rules," rolled back "tough standards on arsenic levels in drinking water," and proposed to "suspend a requirement that miners post a bond to clean up damage to the environment they create." Lobbyists also persuaded Bush to "back away from a pledge to regulate carbon dioxide emissions at power plants." When the new President lowered the federal standard for arsenic in drinking water, he opposed a rule that, according to the *Times*, "would have held miners responsible for the environmental damage they cause on public lands."

Could corporate America ever hope for a more compliant President? Could Republicans ever hope for more collusion from their Democratic "opponents?"

Chapter 11

The Power Game:
"Upside Down and Twisted"

So abused and out of balance with the self-interest of citizens is the lobbying game of 2004 that even Fortune magazine, the periodical of choice for wealthy corporate executives, has reported on it, most recently in an August 2003 article entitled "The Persuaders," by Jeffrey H. Birnbaum, author of the 1994 book, *The Lobbyists: How Influence Peddlers Get Their Way in Washington* (Three Rivers Press).

"When chief executives of American corporations come to Washington," Birnbaum wrote in *Fortune*, "they discover that, to get what they want, they are forced to act in unnatural ways. For instance, nobody at insurance giant American International Group tells CEO Hank Greenberg what to do. He wants to reopen for business in China? Go into the auto insurance game? His people make it so. But when the 78-year-old command-and-control chief comes to Washington, he takes orders from a 36-year-old punk consultant named Mark Isakowitz," a principal of the powerful American Insurance Association (AIA). "If that seems upside down and twisted," Birnbaum continued, "it's because the power structure in Washington is incomprehensibly alien to the businessperson. Power belongs not to the guy at the top, but to the person who knows where to apply pressure – the acupuncturist, if you will. The body politic has numerous pressure points (100 Senators, 435 members in the House, thousands of procedural rules) and the skilled practitioner" knows how to clear the way for his check-bearing clients, quietly and very effectively.

Even if "we the people" wanted to venture to Washington or our statehouses to stand up for our families and communities, how far would we get if *Fortune* is correct in its characterization of the "game?"

It is, in fact, no *game*, and "we the people," minus the corporate interests as privileged entities apart, are paying the price. In the case of corporations, they are *literally* paying the price. "We the people" pay in increasing fiscal sacrifice and a sense of hopelessness.

If we invest even a few minutes of online research on the topic of the iron-fisted alliance between corporations and lobbyists, we will understand, beyond any doubt, that the situation is getting worse rather than better. "Lobbying by companies and their trade associations against social and environmental regulations, or measures to help citizens in poorer countries, is identified as an emerging concern," said the Institute of Environmental Management & Assessment (IEMA) in the United Kingdom in a February 2003 study entitled *Corporate Lobbying Becoming a Key Business Risk.* "Lobbying by companies and their trade associations against social and environmental regulations, or measures to help citizens in poorer countries," the report said, "is identified as an emerging concern." In 2002, IEMA noted in the study, written by lead author Dr. Jem Bendell, "stories about corporate responsibility escaped from environmental and society newspaper columns and landed squarely on the front pages. On the one hand, CEOs went from heroes to zeroes, as corporate governance debacles spread from Enron and

Worldcom to other U.S. companies and then to other parts of the world."

There was, perhaps, a glimpse of hope, Bendell noted. "The United Nations became heavily involved in promoting partnerships for corporate responsibility at the 2nd Earth Summit in Johannesburg, South Africa. The consequences of this increased profile for corporate responsibility will emerge in 2003. As important will be the developments that occurred behind the headlines, as more companies, governments, and civil organizations addressed the role of business in society."

Despite such optimism, global U.S. corporations, and some from elsewhere in major industrialized nations, control the world and everything in it, from what you see – or don't see – on the news, to the standard of living in "developing nations," which increasingly means low-cost job factories that in turn create consumers of mass market American products like Coca-Cola and cigarettes.

But the keys that almost no corporate CEOs or high-priced lobbyists or the governments they influence talk about are the critical parameters of what is called "sustainable growth." What that means, as David C. Korten explained in *When Corporations Rule the World*, is painfully simple: whether the present pace of global business development – labor and consumers in the same human form, expected to be inexhaustible in both capacities – will exhaust the earth's finite resources such as oil, or destroy the environment beyond repair. If you visit the right-wing Republican, pro-George W. Bush web site, *FreeRepublic.com*, you will see the contempt and almost violent hatred held for anyone who professes to want to protect the environment or lift Third World people from the desperation of almost unfathomable poverty.

If that's not bad enough, if you do some more homework you will easily be able to confirm that corporations and their lobbyists and lawyers – often in the same human form – are taking on complex, dangerous issues like increasing the difficulty of bringing lawsuits for the cancers and other human damage associated with things like asbestos poisoning. Leading the way in the asbestos effort is none other than mighty Halliburton, formerly run by Vice President Dick Cheney, and the American Insurance Association, headed by the "36-year-old punk consultant" cited by *Fortune* as one of Washington's most powerful lobbyists.

"Major U.S. corporations from Pfizer to Halliburton are mobilizing scores of public affairs professionals across Washington this fall in hopes that the new legislative session will bring an end to years of costly asbestos-related lawsuits," observed *PR Week*, a public relations magazine, in September 2003. "Working separately as the Asbestos Study Group and the Asbestos Alliance, hundreds of major companies that have either manufactured or used asbestos are lobbying for protection from more than 600,000 asbestos lawsuits now pending in U.S. courts."

To anyone remotely familiar with the physical horrors of asbestos-related cancer, such a huge and well-organized attempt to tilt the balance away from people and toward giant corporations measures up as a crime against humanity. But it is not the worst corporate abuse.

In the most heinous irony of our national victory in the Cold War, our human survival is now threatened by a half-trillion-dollar a year, post-Cold War new business opportunity: the export of death and destruction in the name of "national security." In what will perhaps be the final insult to the interests of the American people, most notably since the national nightmare of 9/11, weaponry and war – cold-blooded profiteering from policy-provoked international mayhem – have become the hotbed of lobbying activity by former U.S. government officials and the most powerful men and women in Washington.

III

The Military-Industrial Complex
& War Profiteering

Chapter 12

The Unknown Soldier: "War is Just a Racket"

On January 17, 1961, outgoing U.S. President Dwight Eisenhower, a legendary military man who had helped mastermind victory in World War II on behalf of America and its allies, made his farewell address to the nation. As the Cold War careened toward the Cuban missile crisis that would lead the world to the brink of nuclear annihilation less than two years later under John F. Kennedy, Eisenhower spoke frankly and presciently to the American people about the undue influence that defense contractors, already feeding at the public trough, were achieving in Washington.

"This conjunction of an immense military establishment and a large arms industry is new in the American experience," Eisenhower declared, with a unique expertise and perspective. "The total influence – economic, political, even spiritual – is felt in every city, every statehouse, every office of the federal government." A few moments later, he issued a stern warning and coined a new term. "In the councils of government, we must guard against the acquisition of unwarranted influence, whether sought or unsought, by the military-industrial complex," Eisenhower said. "The potential for the disastrous rise of misplaced power exists and will persist. We must never let the weight of this combination endanger our liberties or democratic processes. We should take nothing for granted. Only an alert and knowledgeable citizenry can compel the proper meshing of the huge industrial and military machinery of defense with our peaceful methods and goals, so that security and liberty may prosper together."

Three decades earlier, in a little-known speech in 1931, another great American military hero had been even more blunt. "War is just a racket," Marine General Smedley Darlington Butler, a two-time Congressional Medal of Honor winner, said in his own farewell address. "A racket is best described, I believe, as something that is not what it seems to the majority of people. Only a small inside group knows what it is about. It is conducted for the benefit of the very few, at the expense of the masses."

Today, the military-industrial complex – General Butler's "racket" – has spawned what is virtually a secret society of corporate war profiteers, protected by "national security" provisions and top-secret security clearances that prevent "we the people" from having any idea what is really going on.

"There isn't a trick in the racketeering bag that the military gang is blind to," General Butler said. "It has its 'finger men' to point out enemies, its 'muscle men' to destroy enemies, its 'brain men' to plan war preparations, and a 'Big Boss Super-Nationalistic Capitalism' ... I spent 33 years and 4 months in ... the Marine Corps [and] ... I spent most of my time being a high-class muscle man for big business, for Wall Street, and for the bankers. In short, I was a racketeer, a gangster for capitalism."

Despite his cautionary oration, not even Smedley Butler could have foreseen what would happen after the next World War: the institutional merger of military and industrial establishments of which Eisenhower would speak with such concern as he exited the public stage. Almost overnight, a relatively small group of industrialists, investors, and bankers inherited one of the most lucrative business opportunities in

American history: the military run-up to the long nuclear face-off with the Soviet Union.

In the 1960s, the Vietnam War became yet another new business opportunity for the private sector to reap grotesque windfall profits at the expense, both financially and psychologically, of the American people.

With the collapse of the Soviet Union at the end of the 1980s, however, the corporate descendants of the famous World War I "merchants of death" faced a crisis. Their "market" had essentially evaporated. On the political front, "we the people" were promised, all too briefly, a "peace dividend" – lower taxes, increased federal spending on domestic social programs, and a general sense of national well-being – that never materialized. Meanwhile, the military-industrial complex suddenly needed a new enemy, and former President George H. W. Bush, whose family has ranked among the most cold-blooded war profiteers of the last 100 years, conveniently delivered one.

In fact, the stage had already been set. The Bush family and the rest of General Butler's "finger men" and "muscle men" had already discovered a lucrative new niche market. As a result of our nationalistic hatred for Iran following the 1979–80 Iranian hostage crisis, the U.S., between 1985 and 1990, licensed the export of $1.5 billion worth of weaponry, military equipment, and related technology to Iraq, according to arms expert William D. Hartung in his 2003 book *How Much Are You Making On The War, Daddy? A Quick and Dirty Guide to War Profiteering in the Bush Administration* (Nation Books).

By the time Saddam Hussein finally over-stepped a line in the sand, the border to Kuwait in 1990, a half-billion dollars worth of new-generation booty had already been shipped to Iraq, including anthrax, bubonic plague, and other ingredients for chemical and biological weapons. Even Hussein's nuclear weapons program, which would be used in 2003 by George W. Bush as a false and fear-mongering justification for his invasion and occupation of Iraq, was aided and abetted directly by the U.S. government during the Reagan administration.

Even more troubling, perhaps, is the real reason for the rift that erupted between Hussein and George H.W. Bush, the dictator's onetime "ally" and business partner, who, in the long family tradition, has become one of the wealthiest war profiteers in history since leaving office.

Before Hussein invaded Kuwait, Iraqi officials informed then-Assistant U.S. Ambassador to Iraq April Gillespie of his plans, based on age-old disputes over national borders and oil fields. Gillespie told Iraq that the U.S. would have "no position" on such a military incursion. Thinking he had a green light, Hussein went ahead with his invasion – and then saw his former "ally" destroy his country, kill thousands of innocent civilians, and impose decade-long sanctions that, according to the United Nations, led to the deaths of as many as a half-million Iraqi children.

Even before that, the U.S. had betrayed its "ally" during the Reagan administration, when George H.W. Bush served as Vice President. Fighting a difficult and deadly war of attrition against the Iranians, believing America was his friend and supporter against the Ayatollah Khomeini – portrayed in the U.S. as evil incarnate – Hussein was shocked to discover that the U.S. had also been secretly supporting the Iranians, via the infamous Iran-Contra arms deal.

Is it any wonder, then, that Hussein came to mistrust and ultimately despise America?

But what was bad for Hussein and the American troops and innocent Iraqi civilians who were killed, maimed, and disabled, was good for those who profited from the carnage.

Chapter 13

White House or Think Tank: Who's Running Things?

Today, more and more Americans are wondering why the U.S. invaded Iraq in March 2003 and toppled Saddam Hussein. The CIA-connected dictator had done business with the U.S. – and high-ranking former government officials – since the 1970s, via shadowy intermediaries such as the infamous Bank of Credit & Commerce International (BCCI), characterized by investigators as the biggest and most lucrative fraud in history. Among BCCI's well-heeled clientele, in addition to Hussein, were former Panamanian strongman Manuel Noriega, 80s terrorist Abu Nidal, Burmese warlord and raw opiate exporter Khun Sa, close associates of Osama bin Laden, and former President George H.W. Bush.

Clearly, given the public record of the present Bush administration's hypocritical Iraq hyperbole about "gathering danger" and "mushroom clouds," the American people were misled by the senior officials of an entire administration into a war that has increasingly become a military, foreign policy and financial disaster for the United States. In recent months, the Bush administration has even largely abandoned its promise of "freedom and democracy" in Iraq and, instead, become bogged down in a last-ditch attempt to prevent the country from deteriorating into an Islamic state even more hateful of Uncle Sam than Taliban-run Afghanistan had been.

But the question remains: Why did we really go there in the first place?

The answer lies in a report called *Rebuilding America's Defenses*, published in September 2000 – even before George W. Bush got "elected" – by a right-wing, militaristic Washington think tank called Project for the New American Century (PNAC). The well-connected principals of PNAC knew that in light of the end of the Cold War, the U.S. no longer faced any traditional enemy who posed any genuine threat to its national security. PNAC's self-serving objective, then, was to convince the U.S. government, no matter who got elected President, to "project American power" in a new and forceful way that would prevent the near-term emergence of any real, big threat, like a militarized China or a reformed, Communist-leaning Russia. (To read the PNAC report, go to *www.NewAmericanCentury.org/RebuildingAmericasDefenses.pdf*)

It is important to note that the signatories to the PNAC policy manifesto constituted a Bush team in waiting: Vice President Dick Cheney and his top national security assistant, I. Lewis "Scooter" Libby; Secretary of Defense Donald Rumsfeld; Deputy Secretary of Defense Paul Wolfowitz; National Security Council member Elliot Abrams; Undersecretary for Arms Control and International Security John Bolton, and former Chairman of the Defense Policy Board Richard Perle. The PNAC membership roster also included the President of the Committee for the Liberation of Iraq, Randy Scheunemann; Republican Party leader Bruce Jackson, and PNAC chairman William Kristol, conservative writer for *The Weekly Standard*. For good measure, so that the legacy of the "Bush dynasty" might exert its imperial influence into future U.S. Presidential administrations, Jeb

Bush, the president's brother and present governor of Florida, is also a PNAC member.

There could never be a more serious conflict of interests than PNAC between the halls of government and the boardrooms of defense behemoths such as Lockheed Martin, Boeing, and Raytheon. Nevertheless, beyond the inherent conflict and its detriment to the genuine self-interest of "we the people" and the world, there are three very important factors to bear in mind when assessing PNAC and its influence on U.S. military and foreign policy.

The first is that in the afterglow of post-Cold War nationalism, the true nature of these men can be found in the simple fact they called their organization Project for the New *American* Century. If the U.S. truly desired to export "freedom and democracy," as a legacy from our Founding Fathers to the rest of the world, one must wonder why the group didn't call itself Project for the New *World* Century, or New *Human* Century.

The second and even more troubling point is how the pre-George W. Bush exercise in setting military and foreign policy became a verbatim "national security" blueprint for Bush and his PNAC-led military and national security teams. The third point, and perhaps the most telling, in terms of what PNAC's real underlying motive might have been, aside from dangerous ideology and shameless looting of the U.S. Treasury, is the very notion that America's defenses needed to be "rebuilt" in the first place. Since the 1980s, the U.S. has pulverized every "enemy" it has come up against, most notably Iraq in the first Gulf War. In 2003, a second Gulf War was even more of a mismatch in military terms.

Why, then, would any sane "expert" propose that our defenses needed to be "rebuilt?"

The answer lies in a simple but ill-understood truth: that giant corporate war profiteers, like all enterprises, large and small, constantly need new business to stay alive and flourish.

Chapter 14
The "Bush Doctrine": Generations of Blood Money

At the end of the Cold War, top U.S. defense contractors such as Lockheed Martin, Boeing, and Raytheon faced a daunting new challenge: how to avoid anticipated budget cuts as the nation stood down from four decades of increasingly more expensive preparedness for "the final war." In simple terms, President Ronald Reagan had spent so much money on weapons systems and defense-related technologies that he had literally bankrupted the Soviet Union. By the same token, he had poured trillions of taxpayer dollars into American corporate coffers. By the time President George H.W. Bush took office in January 1989, the "evil empire" could no longer hang on in "the arms race."

Peace was at hand.

Peace, however, is bad for the war business, so George Bush I betrayed his old business crony and CIA collaborator Saddam Hussein, and suckered him into the first Gulf War. The extraordinary military capability demonstrated by the United States translated into fast cash for the war profiteers, as global demand for American arms skyrocketed.

When Bush I left office in January 1993, he quickly and quietly cashed in his chips, just as his family had done for generations, going back to World War I under his grandfather, Samuel Bush. In the 1990s, however, George H.W. Bush set a standard that might never be reached again. He joined a super-secret Washington "private equity firm" known as The Carlyle Group. Becoming a "paid advisor" to the $13 billion defense contractor, Bush soon began doing business with his old friends, the Saudis, and the family of Osama bin Laden, with whom the Bushes had done business since the 1970s through a network of intermediaries.

In an explosive book published in August 2004, *Prelude to Terror: The Rise of the Bush Dynasty, the Rogue CIA, and the Compromising of American Intelligence* (Carroll & Graf), intelligence expert Joseph J. Trento documented how an outlaw gang of CIA spymasters, fired by President Jimmy Carter, allied themselves with new Vice President – and former CIA director – George H.W. Bush to create a private intelligence network. That network, led by a maverick CIA operative named Ted Shackley, engineered the Iran-Contra arms-hostages-and-drugs deal and, through the royal family of Saudi Arabia, fostered ties to Islamic terrorists that led inexorably to the attacks of 9/11. Trento's book also revealed how the Bush-led private spy network allowed Osama bin Laden's fundraising to thrive as al Qaeda flourished under the watchful eyes of the CIA and Saudis.

As for the elder Bush's role in The Carlyle Group, the Saudis and their inner circle have, over the years, transacted nearly $1.5 billion in business with the Bush dynasty, according to Craig Unger in his 2004 book, *House of Bush, House of Saud: The Secret Relationship Between the World's Two Most Powerful Dynasties* (Scribner). The deals go back to the scandal-ridden BCCI and Arbusto/Harken Energy, the troubled oil company run by George W. Bush before his ascension to the Presidency.

As for The Carlyle Group, the Saudis have invested $80 million and awarded contracts to Carlyle-controlled companies totaling almost $1.2 billion, according to Unger.

Given Carlyle Group's unique credentials, the Saudis got their money's worth in global influence. Known as "the ex-President's club," the company's inner circle has included George H.W. Bush, former Secretary of State James A. Baker III, former British Prime Minister John Major, and former Secretary of Defense and Deputy Director of the CIA Frank Carlucci, who served as chairman and CEO until 2003.

In turn, The Carlyle Group and the Bush family have invested in or done business with shady "defense contractors" such as anthrax vaccine maker Bio-Port and Engineered Support Systems (ESS), which specializes in high-tech warfare support. An uncle of the current President of the United States sat on the board of ESS prior to Bush's post-9/11 military adventures. The little-known company profited handsomely from "the Bush doctrine."

Such war profiteering shenanigans should not come as a surprise to even a casual student of U.S. defense policy. In the 2002 book, *Into the Buzzsaw: Leading Journalists Expose the Myth of a Free Press* (Prometheus), career journalist turned media critic Carl Jensen – founder of Project Censored, which each year reports the most important unreported, or censored, news stories of the past 12 months – wrote that "the top censored story of 1997 was that the United States was the principal arms merchant for the world." Project Censored warned that "United States troops may be at risk from our own weapons." Today, that very scenario is playing out in Iraq, where U.S. weapons, flak jackets, and military uniforms are on sale, at deeply discounted prices, in downtown Baghdad, according to media reports early in 2004.

That, however, is the least of our problems when it comes to the insidious PNAC and its war-mongering, nationalistic propaganda. The number of policy coincidences the PNAC report has generated is, in fact, uncanny.

George W. Bush's famous "axis of evil" – Iraq, Iran, and North Korea? It came directly from PNAC. The 3.8 percent of gross domestic product (GDP) that the Bush administration ultimately enacted as the minimally acceptable level for defense spending? *Exactly* the amount proposed by PNAC. The militant corporatist prophets of PNAC even came up with the notion of "homeland defense" well before George W. Bush was "elected," and more than a year before the attacks of 9/11.

Chapter 15

The Road to Iraq:
PNAC's Amazing "Pearl Harbor" Prophecy

In June, Medea Benjamin, co-founder of United for Peace & Justice, the largest anti-war coalition in U.S. history, wrote a letter to the American public. Her words illuminate the world "we the people" face today.

"There are many ways to promote peace and justice in our world, but when we face an immediate conflict, indeed a promised 'war without end,' it first helps to step back and look at how it all began," Benjamin observed. "Our current 'War on (some) Terror' was birthed, if not conceived, on September 11, 2001. That day was a terrible funeral pyre for many, but a golden opportunity for some. Only a year before, the Project for the New American Century, a think tank for the Neocon crowd that now controls the White House and the Pentagon, published a martial wish list entitled 'Rebuilding America's Defenses.' Their report outlined our 'urgent need' to inflate defense spending, control Mideast oil, deploy exotic new weapons, and reorganize our forces to fight and win several simultaneous wars. Their stated goal was full spectrum global dominance, a 'Pax Americana,' but they grudged that such a transformation would take forever 'absent some catastrophic and catalyzing event, like a new Pearl Harbor.'

"Consider then all the ignored warnings, quashed investigations, and missing air defenses that preceded 9/11 and gave them this golden opportunity. And post-9/11, consider Condi Rice's chilling remarks: 'Now, we have an opportunity and an obligation to move forward together. Bold and comprehensive changes are sometimes only possible in the wake of catastrophic events ... Just as World War II led to a fundamental reorganization of our national defense structure, so has September 11th made possible sweeping changes in the ways we protect our homeland.'

"Besides pre-emptive wars, September 11th also 'made possible sweeping changes' in the ways the government has stifled our freedoms, enriched corporate backers, attacked the environment, and shredded the social safety net. All these current onslaughts draw their strength from 9/11 and the public's fearful ignorance of what happened on that day. The truth is, we still don't know why we were left so utterly defenseless on 9/11. But before that tragedy is used to justify the death of one more soldier, one more civil liberty, or one more law protecting the environment or the poor, hard questions must be asked."

By the time Benjamin wrote her letter, it was indisputable that the tragedy of 9/11 had become the brazenly exploited *raison d'être* for the Bush administration's unprecedented assaults against two sovereign governments, our national budget, and the Bill of Rights, especially free speech. So effective was Bush's aggressive dogma of "patriotism in a time of war" that the "mainstream" media, and most of the "alternative press," refused to even mention, let alone investigate, the still-unanswered questions about the worst homeland attack in American history. Despite ever-widening holes in the official account of 9/11 events, U.S. news organizations have continued to abet the cover-up and ignore the implications of sobering facts.

There are numerous examples of such media complicity in the 9/11 cover-up, including their staggering indifference to these modestly "newsworthy" facts:

- Victim families, who fought to create the 9/11 Commission, presented it with more than 140 important questions, 90 percent of which remain unanswered to this day.

- Days before 9/11, stock market wagers that United and American Airlines shares would soon crash in value hit an all-time high, and won the prophetic and still-anonymous bettors more than $5 million in illicit spoils.

- The 47-story World Trade Center 7, which was neither hit nor badly damaged, still collapsed with perfect symmetry, from the bottom up, at free-fall speed.

- White House officials – and only White House officials – began taking the antibiotic Cipro on September 11, weeks before the first anthrax threats appeared.

- Pakistan's intelligence chief, who met with former CIA Director George Tenet and other top U.S. officials days before 9/11, sent $100,000 to Mohammed Atta, the alleged lead hijacker, a few weeks earlier.

- Throughout the summer of 2001, top government officials ignored dozens of urgent warnings from foreign governments and stifled FBI field inquiries into al Qaeda operatives.

- FBI whistleblower Sibel Edmonds reported that months before 9/11, she had seen FBI documents warning that al Qaeda was preparing to hit New York with planes. Her efforts to make her findings public have been muzzled by Attorney General John Ashcroft.

- Chairman of the Joint Chiefs of Staff General Richard Myers, a former commander of NORAD, has changed his explanation several times of why U.S. air defenses failed so thoroughly on 9/11.

- No one responsible for ignoring warnings, quashing investigations, or causing our air defense "failures," has ever even been disciplined; in fact, most were promoted to higher posts.

- Former Cabinet ministers in Britain, Germany, and Canada have all publicly stated that the White House's official explanation of our missing air defenses does not stand up to even minimal scrutiny.

- In November 2003, 9/11 widow Ellen Mariani filed a federal RICO (racketeering) suit against the Bush White House for letting 9/11 happen "for personal and political gain."

- On May 26, 2004, *The Toronto Star* reported that 63% of Canadians now believe our government knew 9/11 was coming and didn't interfere. A German poll reached a similar conclusion.

These and scores of other unreported and unexplained facts are currently being brought to public awareness via a growing national network of grassroots organizations such as *911truth.org* and *CooperativeResearch.org*, as well as in authoritative books such as *The New Pearl Harbor: Disturbing Questions About the Bush Administration and 9/11* (Interlink Publishing), by David Ray Griffin, *The War On Freedom: How and Why America Was Attacked on September 11, 2001* (Media Messenger Books) by Nafeez Mosaddeq Ahmed, and *Inside Job* (Origin Press), by best-selling author Jim Marrs.

Meanwhile, back in Iraq, PNAC – also free of press scrutiny – promoted the ascent of now-discredited Iraqi exile Ahmed Chalabi, a convicted bank swindler who headed the CIA-inspired Iraqi National Congress. Not only did Chalabi and his partners in political crime convince the U.S. that

American soldiers would be welcomed with flowers and dancing in the streets; he also received as much as $340,000 a month in U.S. tax dollars for his erroneous, even fraudulent, "insight" into his former homeland and Saddam Hussein's alleged weapons of mass destruction - the trumpeted root cause of the war.

Most dangerously, however, PNAC fostered the notion of a "Pax Americana." Simply put, that means the U.S. must dominate the entire planet, and everyone on it, before a new enemy capable of defending itself against American "hegemony" – such power that our national will cannot be resisted – can muster a "rebuilt" defense of its own. Except for the technology and its inflated 21st century price tag, there is nothing new about such ambitious justification for nationalistic aggression. It used to be called "imperialism," most notably during the Vietnam War.

"Being an imperial power means enforcing such order as there is in the world and doing so in the American interest," Harvard Fellow and author Michael Ignatieff wrote in *The New York Times Magazine* in early January 2003, two months before the U.S. invaded Iraq. "It means laying down the rules America wants ... while exempting itself from other rules that go against its interest."

Other observers provide even more historical context. "Since the late 19th century, the U.S. government has worked aggressively to convince the citizenry of the necessity of going to war in numerous instances," wrote another veteran journalist turned media critic, Robert McChesney, in *Into the Buzzsaw*. "In ... World War I, Korea, Vietnam, and the Gulf War, the government employed sophisticated propaganda campaigns to whip the population into a suitable fury. It was well understood within the establishment at the time – and subsequently verified in historical examinations – that the government needed to lie in order to gain support for its war aims. The media system, in every case, proved to be a superior propaganda organ for militarism and empire."

Not only did McChesney and his fellow *Buzzsaw* contributors soon see such propaganda used to rally Congress and the American people for the 2003 invasion of Iraq, but the manipulative context of the "Bush doctrine" of "pre-emptive" wars could be found in the Nazi rhetoric of Luftwaffe commander Hermann Goering, who observed during the Nuremberg trials: "It is always a simple matter to drag the people along, whether it is a democracy or a fascist dictatorship or a parliament … The people can always be brought to the bidding of the leaders. That is easy. All you have to do is tell them they are being attacked, and denounce the pacifists for lack of patriotism and exposing the country to danger."

Chapter 16

"Peace and Democracy" at the Barrel of a Gun

E xploiting the tragedy of 9/11 to declare his "War on Terror," George W. Bush followed Goering's guideline to the letter. Now the world – and the American people – are beginning to sense the depths of the foreign policy disaster Bush has created and the lies he and his administration have told. A public opinion poll in June 2004 found that 47 percent of the American people felt George W. Bush had "intentionally" misled the U.S. into the Iraq war. Such state subterfuge is nothing new.

In 1917, as the world hurtled toward the first Great War, which would lead to human carnage on a scale never seen before, the great American writer and social critic Mark Twain made an observation in *The Mysterious Stranger* that rings with truth today. "Next," Twain wrote, "the statesmen will invent cheap lies, putting the blame upon the nation that is attacked, and every man will be glad of those conscience-soothing falsities, and will diligently study them, and refuse to examine any refutations of them; and thus he will, by and by, convince himself that the war is just, and will thank God for the better sleep he enjoys after this process of grotesque self-deception."

Today, "we the people" must address the fact that the Bush administration went to war largely because PNAC lobbied for the U.S. to leverage its new post-Cold War status as "the world's singular superpower ... to spread its influence into geographic areas that are ideologically opposed to our influence."

In addition, with a sort of *Dr. Strangelove* logic, PNAC promoted the theory, says anti-PNAC activist Bette Stockbauer, that "the only way to preserve peace in the coming era will be to increase military forces for the purpose of waging multiple wars to subdue countries which may stand in the way of U.S. global preeminence."

To understand what is actually going on in our names, whether we support it or not, we must fully comprehend the ideological origins of PNAC. In a larger context, it is part of a right-wing Christian-Neocon movement that seeks U.S. dominance of the earth – all its countries, resources, and people – in the name of God.

Despite anti-Muslim western propaganda to the contrary, radical Islamists – the "evildoers" of the Bush-Neocon lexicon – do not share the same goal as Christian neo-crusaders. The primary difference is that the U.S.-based Christian-militarist right has most of the money and the weapons, as well as the institutional and enlisted manpower.

"The Neocon Christians may want to take over the world," Enver Masud, an award-winning author and founder-CEO of the Washington, DC-based Muslim educational foundation The Wisdom Fund, said in an interview for this book, "but al Qaeda and other Muslims merely want the U.S. to stop meddling in their world and standing in the way of a just resolution of the Israeli-Palestinian conflict."

Masud also makes another important distinction between Muslims and conversion-obsessed Christians. "Muslims begin everything in the name of Allah: eat lunch, start a journey, begin a speech, and so on," he explains. "But it is not the same as right-wing Christians wanting to bring God to the 'heathens.' Informed Muslims are aware of the Koran's injunction against compelling one's faith on another. Indeed, the Koran is quite explicit that there have been many prophets who have taught different paths to the One God, whether called Yahweh or Allah."

For their part, the militarist right-wing Christians "are no tiny band of cranks meeting in some basement in Alabama," journalist Chris Floyd reported last March in the online journal *Global Eye*. "[They] are bankrolled and directed by deep-pocketed, well-connected business moguls and political operatives who have engineered a takeover of the Republican Party and are now at the heart of the U.S. government. They've made common cause with the 'American Empire' faction – Cheney, Rumsfeld, the Neoconservatives – who seek 'full-spectrum dominance' over the globe."

In effect, then, PNAC policy initiatives on behalf of the Neocon Christian elites constitute a shadow government that not only sees itself as above the law and answerable to a "higher authority," but professes to believe it is on a mission from our Creator Himself. In its righteous zeal, PNAC also pushed for increased ability to fight "big wars" and to conduct more than one "large-scale war" at the same time. In the aftermath of such large wars fought simultaneously, PNAC suggested, the U.S. must be ready to use its military might to perform "constabulary duties" – meaning, in effect, to be a military police force for the entire globe.

That means that, in essence, the U.S. will use its military power to enforce its self-serving, nationalistic policy initiatives in every country on earth where we either face ideological opposition or require resources, such as oil and gas.

To provide a sobering context for that point, Uncle Sam presently has troops in more than 130 of the 191 member nations of the UN.

Chapter 17

Is What's Good for Boeing Good for America?

"Under post-Cold War U.S. 'leadership,' the country – and the world – have gone insane," says 89-year-old John McConnell, the founder of Earth Day in 1970 and the Minute for Peace, which officially ended the period of national mourning after the assassination of John F. Kennedy in 1963. During his lifetime, McConnell's friends have included 33 Nobel laureates and three Secretaries-General of the UN. "Building more and more efficient technologies for killing is inhuman. So is the militarization and arming of space. We have to stop the madness before the madness ends life on earth."

Anti-PNAC activist Bette Stockbauer has spoken out with a more practical sentiment. "Their flaws in logic are obvious to people of conscience," she wrote. "Namely, that a combative posture on our part will not secure peace, but will rather engender fear throughout the world and begin anew the arms race, only this time with far more contenders, and that democracy, by its very definition, cannot be imposed by force."

In fact, to anyone who makes a careful study of 20th century U.S. military history and the private financial forces behind it, the imposition of democracy and freedom are the antithesis of the real goal: instability and chaos that create new business opportunities, expanded markets, for the war profiteers.

"When President Eisenhower sounded his famous warning about the dangers posed to our democracy by the military-industrial complex, he couldn't have imagined the ruthless efficiency this political machinery would be put to in the era of Karl Rove, Donald Rumsfeld, and The Carlyle Group," William D. Hartung wrote in the preface to his book, *How Much Are You Making On The War, Daddy?* "Currently, President George W. Bush – a self-described 'compassionate conservative' who vowed to pursue a 'humble' foreign policy – presides over a vastly expanded national security state that bears little resemblance to the government he took control of [in 2001]."

While state and local governments struggle with their worst fiscal crises since World War II, according to a 2002 report by the National Governors Association and the National Association of State Budget Officers, and the Bush administration continues to slash costs from domestic budgets almost across the board in 2004, the big beneficiaries of Bush's "endless" War on Terror are the giant corporate militarists, who have enjoyed huge increases in spending since 9/11.

"If the administration's strategy of using force and the threat of force as its primary tools for dealing with terrorists and tyrants is fully implemented," Hartung wrote in his February 2003 report for the Freedom Forum, "these new expenditures may just be the down payment on a long-term buildup that will push U.S. military spending to Cold War levels and beyond. Based on current Pentagon spending projections, U.S. military spending will total $4.3 trillion during this decade, with annual spending on national defense topping $500 billion per year by 2009."

Hartung and others have noted, however, that the runaway spending has almost no relevance to the real threat facing America: stateless international terrorists organized into anonymous cells, in countries all over the world. "As a recent analysis by Steven M. Kosiak of the Center for Strategic and Budgetary Assessments has demonstrated," Hartung wrote in his report just prior to the Iraq invasion, "only about one third of the Pentagon's increased funding between fiscal year [FY] 2001 and FY 2003 has been devoted to homeland security and combating terrorism, and only 5 to 10 percent of the Pentagon's total budget for FY 2003 is being set aside for these purposes."

In addition, Hartung explained, "one of the greatest potential costs of relying on war and preparations for war as a centerpiece of U.S. foreign policy is the danger of distorting the U.S. role in the world from that of a vibrant democracy that is ready to defend itself and its allies when necessary, to that of a garrison state that uses force to get its way on a wide range of issues that have little to do with self-defense."

Hartung, too, then invoked Mark Twain, a passionate anti-imperialist, who said nearly a hundred years ago, "When the only tool you have is a hammer, all your problems start to look like nails."

In a related context, the late former President Eisenhower also noted the human cost of the military-industrial complex more than 40 years ago: "Every gun that is made, every warship launched, every rocket fired," Eisenhower said, "signifies, in the final sense, a theft from those who hunger and are not fed, those who are cold and not clothed."

To provide some contemporary context for Eisenhower's point, "the proposed Pentagon budget of $399 billion for FY 2004 is more than five times the annual cost of shoring up Social Security," Hartung noted in his Freedom Forum report. In a February 2004 article, "Is What's Good for Boeing and Halliburton Good for America?" – published by the Arms Trade Resource Center – Hartung and his associates Michelle Ciarrocca and Frida Berrigan noted that

three of the Pentagon's biggest defense contractors –
Lockheed Martin, Boeing, and Northrup Grumann – "alone
split over $50 billion in prime contracts ... in FY 2003. To
put this in some perspective, Lockheed Martin's Pentagon
awards, at $21.9 billion, are greater in value than the entire
budget for the federal government's largest single welfare
program, Temporary Assistance for Needy Families, which is
meant to keep several million single parents and dependent
children out of poverty."

Meanwhile, Hartung pointed out – while as many as two
million Americans, including women and children, remain
homeless under the reign of George W. Bush and millions
more sink below the poverty line while working full-time at
minimum-wage jobs – "public awareness of the costs and
risks involved in military intervention has waned. This is an
unhealthy trend in a democracy, particularly one which is
poised at the brink of a new era which may involve much
more frequent military intervention under a series of much
riskier scenarios."

Given the policy initiatives of Project for the New
American Century, the fiscal agenda of multi-billion-dollar
war profiteers such as Halliburton, and the lobbying clout of
some of Washington's most powerful insiders – who daily
support the dynamic duo of interrelated preceding causes –
perhaps "we the people" will soon begin to understand the
long-term social and political consequences of what is
happening right before our eyes.

Chapter 18

Voices of Sanity: On the Outside Looking In

How has the insane U.S. defense policy been so easily perpetrated against the people of America and the world? It has been bought and paid for with campaign contributions and reinforced with the rhetorical leverage of "patriotism."

"In 2000," defense analyst Michelle Ciarrocca of the Arms Trade Resource Center noted in a September 2002 report in *Foreign Policy in Focus*, the six biggest U.S. defense contractors "spent over $6.5 million in contributions to candidates and political parties. In addition to these hefty campaign donations, defense contractors spent an astonishing $60 million on lobbying in 2000." Moreover, Ciarrocca noted, there is a "revolving door that rewards senior military leaders with the promise of future civilian employment if they 'play the game.' "

In the meantime, the post-Gulf War I export of American arms has made U.S. war profiteers fat and powerful beyond imagination. In fairness to the Bush administration, the massive sales actually began under former President Bill Clinton. According to a 1997 report from *The Bulletin of*

Atomic Scientists, international arms sales totaled more than $120 billion a year. As usual, the report noted, U.S. arms merchants had manipulated Congress, to the detriment of the people. "Nearly 6,400 Pentagon, State, and Commerce Department employees are assigned full-time to help arms makers promote, broker, negotiate, and close foreign sales," the report noted. "The government spends an estimated $7.5 billion a year to support weapons merchants through a mixture of grants, subsidized loans, tax breaks, and promotional activities ... Arms exporters' subsidies are now second only to agricultural price support ... Arms exports through the end of [the 1990s] will be paid for by the U.S. taxpayer, not by foreign weapons buyers," the scientific bulletin reported.

Today, the numbers are even worse for taxpayers.

Even more alarmingly, perhaps, according to investigative journalism magazine *Mother Jones,* the U.S. "also has a nasty habit of arming both sides in a conflict, as well as countries with blighted democracy or human rights records, like Indonesia, Colombia, and Saudi Arabia." At the same time, such sales often cause the same social damage to our "allies" that Eisenhower warned about on the domestic front. "Despite government assurances that exports are carefully vetted," the report in *The Bulletin of Atomic Scientists* revealed, "over the last four years 84 percent of U.S. arms transfers to the developing world have gone to countries the State Department considers undemocratic. In addition, U.S. weapons are involved in 45 of the world's 50 largest ethnic and territorial conflicts. Not only do these weapons increase global insecurity, they can turn around and become a threat to U.S. forces stationed overseas.

"As Oscar Arias, a Nobel Peace Prize laureate and champion of arms export controls, has often said," the scientific bulletin observed, "countries beset with poverty deprive their citizens of basic human and civil rights when they spend precious resources on deadly weapons. Turkey, for instance, has a weak economy and a bloated military, and gets many weapons from the United States – either as giveaways or purchases made with U.S. taxpayer-backed loan guarantees. It has turned those weapons against the Kurdish population of southeastern Turkey, where 3,000 villages have been bombed."

Is it any wonder, then, that the Turkish people rose up and demanded – successfully – that their government decline to provide military bases for the U.S. invasion of Iraq? In its never-ending hypocrisy, U.S. administrations blame others – like Saddam Hussein for the murder of Kurds – when our "allies" perpetrate identical crimes against humanity with American-made weapons.

Nevertheless, the Turkish rejection was one of the few setbacks suffered by the PNAC-inspired militarists of the Bush administration in its relentless quest for Pax Americana. With Washington's most powerful former government insiders engaged via private "equity funds" such as The Carlyle Group, and some of the capital's most influential lobbyists on the payrolls of big defense contractors, the Bush administration can do whatever it pleases in the world, according to independent defense analysts such as Ciarrocca and Hartung.

Fortunately, however, there are sane minds at work on U.S. defense policy. The problem is that they are on the outside looking in, and the corporate-controlled media – today not much more than a propaganda machine for outfits like PNAC and similarly dangerous militaristic ideologues – give them little, if any, voice in the debate.

Chris Hellman, a respected analyst for the Council for a Livable World, is a former policy analyst with the Center for Defense Information. Hellman noted, in an interview for this book, that in the post-Iraq world of 2004, the U.S. still has a huge, cumbersome, overly expensive military designed to fight a cataclysmic land war against the former Soviet Union. Despite PNAC's self-serving characterization to the contrary, Hellman says the U.S. has plenty of military muscle to defeat, even obliterate, any global foe – present or future. He also says the defense budget could be cut by 25 percent, or even more, without putting America at risk.

Morton Goulder, who served as Deputy Assistant Secretary of Defense for Intelligence and Warning under Presidents Nixon, Ford, and Carter, agreed with Hellman's assessment in an interview for this book. "The size of the defense budget today has a lot more to do with the defense of corporate profits and Congressional seats than the defense of the country," says Goulder, who worked private-sector defense contractor stints before and after his Pentagon tenures. "We could cut the entire Pentagon budget by a hundred billion dollars a year, if not more, without affecting our real national security at all."

The current political problem, Hellman says, is that "in Washington, you'd better not be parroted as 'soft on defense.' That mentality has really been reinforced since 9/11, so it's hard to even get a debate on the issue. The other problem is that the way the military budget is set up now, you can't even discuss significant cuts without analyzing what our capabilities are and what they need to be." The final – and perhaps most damaging – consideration, Hellman observes, is that "until 9/11 and its aftermath, the entire debate was inside the Beltway in Washington."

Hellman, Goulder, Hartung, and many other defense analysts and social policymakers hope that reality is changing and that the average American will become educated about and involved in such debate, which now affects the future of every U.S. citizen, regardless of political or social stripe.

Chapter 19

Bush Doctrine II: Endless War, Endless Lies

Aside from U.S. Marine General Smedley Butler, the two-time Congressional Medal of Honor winner who called war a "racket" during his 1931 retirement speech, American writer Emma Goldman – another discarded voice of conscience in the dustbin of history – ranks high on the list of those relatively few Americans who have risked everything to expose harsh, ignored truth.

An anarchist-organizer who fought for worker's rights, women's rights, and civil rights long before they became fashionable causes and made headlines in reputable newspapers, Goldman was immortalized as a fierce populist in dozens of books and in Warren Beatty's Academy Award-winning 1981 film, *Reds*.

In 1911, in a then-scandalous but since long-forgotten essay, "Patriotism: A Menace to Liberty," still revered by peace activists around the world, Goldman wrote: "We Americans claim to be a peace-loving people. We hate bloodshed; we are opposed to violence. Yet we go into spasms of joy over the possibility of projecting dynamite bombs from flying machines upon helpless citizens ... Our hearts swell with pride at the thought that America is becoming the most powerful nation on earth, and that it will eventually plant her iron foot on the necks of all other nations. Such is the logic of patriotism."

In 2004 America, "we the people" must come to understand, and admit, the illogic and fear-mongering of right-wing militarists born of a bond of "patriotic" belligerence between the Project for the New American Century (PNAC), the Neocon Christians, and the corporate-controlled mass media. Despite their propaganda to the contrary, they are sinister forces rather than good, and their entire strategy for global hegemony is based on lies rather than truth.

"If you tell a lie big enough and keep repeating it," Nazi Minister of Propaganda Joseph Goebbels once observed, "people will eventually come to believe it."

George W. Bush's big lie, the one he and senior members of his administration have clung to despite mounting evidence to the contrary, has been that the U.S. invasion and occupation of Iraq were justified by Iraqi weapons of mass destruction and a looming nuclear threat that could unleash a "mushroom cloud" on the U.S. Both claims have turned out to be false. In their conspiracy to support their premise, Bush and his cronies told a never-ending series of lies that have now been documented.

In March 2004, a year after the U.S. invasion of Iraq, U.S. Representative Henry Waxman, a California Democrat and one of the few heroes left in Congress, released a report that cited a total of 237 "misleading statements" by the President and his top advisers. In diplomatic-speak, "misleading statement" is a slightly more polite way of saying something is a lie.

The important thing about the Waxman report is that its conclusions about Bush administration lies are based on the public record – speeches made or TV appearances videotaped, both before and since the invasion – measured against the interpretations and statements of the U.S.

intelligence community, both before and since the administration's "misleading statements" were made.

"On March 19, 2003, U.S. forces began military operations in Iraq," the Waxman report, titled *Iraq on the Record*, begins. "Addressing the nation about the purpose of the war on the day the bombing began, President Bush stated: 'The people of the United States and our friends and allies will not live at the mercy of an outlaw regime that threatens the peace with weapons of mass murder.'"

"The *Iraq on the Record* database contains 237 misleading statements about the threat posed by Iraq that were made by President Bush, Vice President Cheney, Secretary Rumsfeld, Secretary Powell, and National Security Advisor Rice," the Waxman report continues. "These statements were made in 125 separate appearances, consisting of 40 speeches, 26 press conferences and briefings, 53 interviews, 4 written statements, and 2 Congressional testimonies. Most of the statements in the database were misleading because they expressed certainty where none existed or failed to acknowledge the doubts of intelligence officials. Ten of the statements were simply false."

It must be underscored that on two occasions, senior members of the Bush administration misled Congress. Yet, a Republican-controlled Congress – much like the one that impeached Bill Clinton for lying about sex – has refused to investigate Bush lies that have led to countless deaths, including nearly 1,000 American troops and an unknown number of innocent Iraqi civilians.

"The 30-day period with the greatest number of misleading statements was the period before the Congressional vote on the Iraq war resolution," *Iraq on the Record* goes on. "Congress voted on the measure on October 10 and October 11, 2002. From September 8 through October 8, 2002, the five officials made 64 misleading statements in 16 public appearances. A large number of misleading statements were also made during the two months before the war began. Between January 19 and March 19,

2003, the five officials made 48 misleading statements in 26 public appearances."

Chapter 20

Tom Paine: "The Irresistible Nature of Truth"

W hy is the little-known Waxman report – not addressed by any major media coverage since its release – so important?

"The President and his senior advisors have a special obligation to describe accurately the national security threats facing the nation," the report says. "There is no decision ... more grave than sending our armed forces to battle. The special obligation also derives in part from the unique access that the President and his advisors have to classified information. On matters of national security, *only the President and his advisors* [emphasis added] have full access to the relevant classified information. Members of Congress and the public see only a partial picture based on the information the President and his advisors decide to release."

It is precisely, and only, as a result of the manipulation, or outright misrepresentation, of such classified information that "we the people" of 2004, living in "the information age" of instant global communication, can be so misled.

As for President Bush, he personally set the standard for the brazen barrage of "misleading" anti-Iraq propaganda that allegedly justified his unprecedented U.S. war of "pre-emption."

"Between September 12, 2002, and July 17, 2003," *Iraq on the Record* reports, "President Bush made 55 misleading statements about the threat posed by Iraq in 27 separate public appearances. On October 7, 2002, three days before the Congressional votes on the Iraqi war resolution, President Bush gave a speech in Cincinnati, Ohio, with 11 misleading statements, *the most by any of the five officials in a single appearance.*" [emphasis added].

On October 7, 2002, the President made a terrifying statement about Saddam Hussein's capabilities and intentions in public remarks at the White House: "We've also discovered through intelligence that Iraq has a growing fleet of manned and unmanned aerial vehicles [UAVs] that could be used to disperse chemical or biological weapons across broad areas. We are concerned that Iraq is exploring ways of using these UAVs for missions targeting the United States." *Iraq on the Record* reports that Bush "failed to mention" that the U.S. government agency most knowledgeable about UAVs and their potential applications – the Air Force's National Air and Space Intelligence Center – publicly rejected the President's assessment. In fact, the wood, wire, and tin "UAVs" looked more like Rube Goldberg prototypes than anything that could threaten the U.S.

On May 29, 2003, Bush proclaimed, in an interview with Polish TV at the White House, "We found the weapons of mass destruction. We found biological laboratories ... We'll find more weapons as time goes on. But for those who say we haven't found the banned manufacturing devices or banned weapons, they're wrong. We found them." The Waxman report explains that Bush failed to disclose the fact that "engineers from the Defense Intelligence Agency who examined the mobile trailers allegedly used to manufacture WMD concluded ... they were most likely used to produce hydrogen for artillery weather balloons."

Not to be outdone, the report noted, Vice President Dick Cheney, "between March 17, 2002, and January 22, 2004 ... made 51 misleading statements about the threat posed by Iraq in 25 separate public appearances ... Secretary Rumsfeld made 52 misleading statements ... in 23 separate public statements or appearances ... Secretary Powell made 50 misleading statements ... in 34 separate public statements or appearances ... Rice made 29 misleading statements ... in 16 separate public statements or appearances."

To read the entire report, go to *www.house.gov/reform/min/features/iraq_on_the_record.*

In conclusion, *Iraq on the Record* explained, "Because of the gravity of the subject and the President's unique access to classified information, members of Congress and the public expect the President and his senior officials to take special care to be balanced and accurate in describing national security threats. It does not appear, however, that President Bush, Vice President Cheney, Secretary Rumsfeld, Secretary Powell, and National Security Advisor Rice met this standard in the case of Iraq. To the contrary, these five officials repeatedly made misleading statements about the threat posed by Iraq. In 125 separate appearances, they made 11 misleading statements about the urgency of Iraq's threat, 81 misleading statements about Iraq's nuclear activities, 84 misleading statements about Iraq's chemical and biological capabilities, and 61 misleading statements about Iraq's relationship with al Qaeda."

The fear-mongering intensity of such subterfuge and deceit would have appalled our Founding Fathers – and it should appall the Congress and American people today.

"Such is the irresistible nature of truth," Thomas Paine wrote in *The Rights of Man, II* in 1792, "that all it asks, and all it wants, is the liberty of appearing." Thomas Jefferson offered a companion thought in 1795: "There is but one straight course, and that is to seek truth and pursue it steadily."

By such lofty standards of honor, "we the people" have failed to live up to our heritage. What have we – or Congress – done to hold the President accountable?

Our silence makes us accomplices in the carnage. Our willingness to allow institutional deceit at the highest levels of government makes us complicit in the eyes of the rest of the world.

Chapter 21

America as "The Greatest Danger to World Peace"

The corporate-controlled mass media never made an issue of the Waxman report. Major newspapers, including *The New York Times* and *Washington Post*, ignored it, as did the big three TV networks and major cable news outlets such as Fox and CNN. Meanwhile, with his lies protected by a cowardly Congress and compliant media – and, as a result, unknown to a mostly still-ignorant public at large – George W. Bush has embodied a remark made 200 years ago by Samuel Johnson: "Patriotism is the last refuge of a scoundrel."

The situation – a genuine national crisis, as yet unleashed by widespread public knowledge – brings to mind another passage from Emma Goldman's pre-World War I essay on patriotism. "Leo Tolstoy, the greatest anti-patriot of our times," Goldman noted, "defines patriotism as the principle that will justify the training of wholesale murderers; a trade that requires better equipment for the exercise of man-killing than the making of such necessities of life as shoes, clothing, and houses; a trade that guarantees better returns and greater glory than that of the average workingman."

Today, more than ever, those sentiments ring with truth and relevance. They expose the underlying inhumanity of corporate and ideological thugs such as Project for the New American Century, America's biggest defense contractors, and the Neocon Christians who purport to justify U.S. hegemony in the name of God. "Conceit, arrogance, and egotism are the essentials of patriotism," Goldman declared. "Patriotism assumes that our globe is divided into little spots, each one surrounded by an iron gate. Those who have had the fortune of being born on some particular spot consider themselves better, nobler, grander, more intelligent than the living beings inhabiting any other spot. It is, therefore, the duty of everyone living on that chosen spot to fight, kill, and die in the attempt to impose his superiority upon all the others."

In an April 2004 essay in *The New Statesman* in the United Kingdom, acclaimed journalist, author and documentary filmmaker John Pilger invoked an immutable truth in a way Emma Goldman would have approved. " 'What we do routinely in the imperial west,' Pilger quoted Richard Falk, professor of international relations at Princeton University, as saying, 'is propagate through a self-righteous, one-way moral/legal screen positive images of western values and innocence that are threatened, validating a campaign of unrestricted violence.' Thus, western state terrorism is erased, and a tenet of western journalism is to excuse or minimize 'our' culpability, however atrocious. Our dead are counted; theirs are not. Our victims are worthy; theirs are not."

The result of such inhumanity to our fellow men of a different religion, or different political ideology, or conflicting foreign policy initiative, is to create what Egyptian President Hosni Mubarak called in April 2004 the most unprecedented and extreme "hatred of America in the Arab world" he could remember from his long political career. In a spring 2004 appearance on the CBS Sunday morning program *Face the*

Nation, U.S. Senator Carl Levin went even further, noting that the hatred of the U.S. by the leaders and citizens of our traditional allies is at an all-time high.

Enver Masud, CEO of the Muslim education organization The Wisdom Fund and author of *The War on Islam*, has cited a 2003 survey in the European edition of *Time* that asked: "Which country really poses the greatest danger to world peace in 2003?"

"With 673,027 votes cast," Masud noted, "the results as of March 10, 2003, were North Korea 5.6 percent; Iraq 6.5 percent; the United States 87.9 percent."

Can anyone really be surprised, then, that hatred for America and Americans is growing, like a cancer, on a daily basis?

"It is only defensive war that can be justified in the sight of God," pre-American Revolution minister Simeon Howard preached to the Ancient and Honorable Artillery Company on June 7, 1773. "When no injury is offered us, we have no right to molest others ... Christian meekness, patience, and forbearance are duties that ought to be practiced both by kingdoms and individuals ... Both religion and humanity strongly forbid the bloody deeds of war, unless they are necessary."

"If there is a sin superior to every other it is that of willful and offensive war," Thomas Paine wrote in 1778 in *The Crisis*. "He who is the author of a war lets loose the whole contagion of hell and opens a vein that bleeds a nation to death."

Two years later, Benjamin Franklin suggested that men should become "convinced that even successful wars at length become misfortunes to those who unjustly commenced them, and who triumphed blindly in their success, not seeing all the consequences."

In *Madison's Warnings on War* in 1795, James Madison observed, "Of all the enemies to public liberty, war is, perhaps, the most to be dreaded, because it comprises and develops the germ of every other. War is the parent of armies;

from these proceed debts and taxes; and armies, and debts, and taxes are the known instruments for bringing the many under the domination of the few ... No nation could preserve its freedom in the midst of continual warfare."

Chapter 22

The Sorrows of Empire:
Truth as "Enemy of the State"

To anyone who takes a moment to indulge in free, honest thought, it has to be troubling that as Iraqis rose to defend their "spot" on the planet in a legitimate, if brutally violent, insurgency against U.S. occupation, George W. Bush and his mass media mouthpieces condemned them as "terrorists, thugs, and assassins." Under any basic measure of international law or sense of history, who can say that the native population of a country has no right to defend itself against a foreign invader?

But in their ever-wider grasp for the big lie that will stick, Bush, Cheney, Rumsfeld, Powell, and Rice insist they are battling "evildoers" and "barbarians" in "the central theater of the war on terror." The only problem with such claims is that like all their others, they are contrary to fact.

There were no terrorists in Iraq – except an aging, infirmed Abu Nidal, a relic of the 1980s and a former Bush family business associate via BCCI – until the U.S. invaded.

Today, on a worldwide basis, there are more terrorist organizations and more attacks than there were before 9/11.

Since that terrible day, more innocent people, including Americans, have died more violently at the hands of terrorists than before. Meanwhile, al Qaeda, according to independent experts, has become stronger and better organized, not weaker and "on the run," as President Bush and Vice President Cheney have repeatedly claimed in yet another series of fabrications.

In June, an admittedly "embarrassed" Secretary of State Colin Powell had to face TV cameras and acknowledge that his department's annual report on international terrorism had grossly misreported the truth: that since 9/11 worldwide death and injury from terrorist attacks have more than doubled. The original version had claimed terrorism had been significantly reduced. The Bush administration blamed the misstatement of fact on a clerical error.

A more important truth, however, has escaped media scrutiny and public awareness. With its imperialistic, PNAC-inspired invasions of Iraq and Afghanistan, the Neocon-run Bush administration saw a no-lose situation in the long run. Either the unprecedented U.S. militarism would create a new geopolitical presence in the oil- and gas-rich region, or it would create the international instability and perpetual warfare from which the Bush family has profited for 100 years. In the former instance, Bush would deliver a secure business platform for his Halliburton and Carlyle Group cronies. In the latter, he would foment global chaos that would help PNAC and the Neocons demonize yet another "new enemy" that allegedly threatens the U.S. Either way, there would be plenty of money to be made, with only the American people and U.S. Treasury as losers.

Meanwhile, in Afghanistan, CIA-paid tribal warlords turned opium barons are the de facto rulers of 80 percent of the country. President Hamid Karzai, a former Chevron operative turned U.S. puppet in the eyes of many Afghans and world leaders, admitted as much on NBC's *Meet the Press* in late May 2004. The UN has reported in recent months that the Afghan experiment in Bush-exported "freedom and democracy" teeters on the verge of collapse, as only a small percentage of the country's eligible voters have registered and Taliban forces are once again on the rise.

In Iraq – despite our self-image as "the world's only superpower" – we are about to face another disastrous loss, just as we did in Vietnam, says University of California-San Diego professor Chalmers Johnson, author of *The Sorrows of Empire: Militarism, Secrecy and the End of the Republic* (Metropolitan Books, 2004). The blow to the psyche of our country and our armed forces will soon be felt, Johnson predicted in late April 2004 in an interview on C-SPAN. "No one wants to be killed in a lost cause," he said. "We are going to lose in Iraq, and there's no doubt about it."

In addition, we are no safer now than we were before we invaded Afghanistan and Iraq. In fact, according to a growing number of terrorism experts and former government officials, we are far less secure. Public opinion polls have confirmed that an increasing number of Americans feel less safe.

For that simple reason – and his administration's more than 200 lies about Iraq – George W. Bush will eventually comprehend the truth of a famous precept of Joseph Goebbels, the brilliant Nazi propagandist: "The lie can be maintained only for such time as the state can shield the people from the political, economic, and military consequences of the lie. It thus becomes vitally important for the state to use all its powers to repress dissent, for the truth is the mortal enemy of the lie – and thus by extension, the truth becomes the greatest enemy of the state."

IV

The Rise of Religion & Theocracy

Chapter 23

George W. Bush:
"God's Man" in the White House

To the many millions of Americans who still believe the U.S. Supreme Court "selected" George W. Bush as President in 2000, as opposed to his being "elected" by voters, it might come as a surprise to discover that Bush's most ardent and outspoken supporters agree with their characterization of the outcome. It will probably also come as a surprise – hopefully a very troubling one – that the right-wing militarist Neocons who populate Bush's core base of support believe that an even higher authority than the nation's High Court did the selecting. Neocon ideologues, from Congress to the courts, from the ivory towers of media moguls to Sunday morning pulpits, believe that God put Bush in the White House.

Given the horrific role of Christian extremism in world and U.S. history, it would be good for the average American to understand the extent to which the Bush administration has made religious fundamentalism a political tactic. "If the Presidency is a 'bully pulpit' as Teddy Roosevelt claimed," Stephen Mansfield wrote in the introduction to his largely approving 2003 book, *The Faith of George W. Bush* (Jeremy P. Tarcher), "no one in recent memory has pounded that pulpit for religion's role in government quite like the 43rd President."

Another journalist and author, Katherine Yurica, has, with her daughter, posted a profoundly important and informative web site (*www.yuricareport.com*) that explains the unprecedented religiosity of the Bush administration. For 20 years, Yurica has reported extensively on the role of religion in public life, based on careful analysis of the TV ministries of right-wing Christian ideologues such as Pat Robertson.

In a well-reported February 2004 essay entitled "The Despoiling of America: The First Prince of the Theocratic States of America," Yurica detailed the Bush doctrine for a theocracy – a form of government in which God or a deity is recognized as the supreme civil ruler – in America. The brutal Taliban of Afghanistan reigned as a textbook theocracy, based on a radical and violent interpretation of Muslim scriptures.

Yurica, who wrote a prescient book two decades ago called *The New Messiahs*, is uniquely qualified for her present task. Her extensive study of 1,300 pages of transcripts from 1980s TV shows hosted by Robertson has been validated by the Subcommittee on Oversight of the House Ways and Means Committee, which ultimately published Yurica's study in *Federal Tax Rules Applicable to Tax-Exempt Organizations Involving Television Ministries* (1988).

Given her expertise and established credentials, Yurica made a troubling new revelation when she reported that the sinister, imperialistic doctrine of U.S. global hegemony in the name of God had quietly assumed a name adapted from Christian scripture: Dominionism.

It means, quite simply, the domination – by force if necessary – of the entire world, and everyone in it, in the name of Jesus Christ. It also means that Biblical law will supercede modern civil law.

"Dominionism," Yurica explained in her essay, "is a natural if unintended extension of Social Darwinism, and is frequently called 'Christian Reconstructionism.' Its doctrines are shocking to ordinary Christian believers and to most Americans. Journalist Frederick Clarkson, who has written extensively on the subject, warned in 1994 that Dominionism 'seeks to replace democracy with a theocratic elite that would govern by imposing their interpretation of Biblical law.' "

The ultimate aims of Dominionism, Yurica explained, are to eliminate labor unions, civil rights laws, and public schools. Anyone who considers such a prediction paranoid might want to consider that since the Bible-thumping Bush administration took office, the membership rosters of major labor unions have dwindled, Constitutional rights and civil liberties have eroded under the Patriot Act, and the Southern Baptist Convention and other right-wing religious groups have publicly campaigned for Christians to remove their children from public schools.

"It is estimated that 35 million Americans who call themselves Christian adhere to Dominionism in the United States," Yurica wrote, "but most of these people appear to be ignorant of the heretical nature of their beliefs and the seditious nature of their political goals. So successfully have the televangelists and churches inculcated the idea of the existence of an outside 'enemy,' which is attacking Christianity, that millions of people have perceived themselves rightfully overthrowing an imaginary evil anti-Christian conspiratorial secular society."

Dominionism is the creation of the late R.J. Rushdoony, the son of Armenian immigrants and an ordained minister in the Orthodox Presbyterian Church, who spent his early career as a missionary on Native American reservations. His 1973 book, *The Institutes of Biblical Law*, laid the groundwork for an obsessively self-righteous and wrathful doctrine that evolved into the philosophy of Dominionism. Rushdoony's son-in-law, Gary North, now helps guide and shape the growing movement of "true believers."

Its most fanatical adherents include Pat Robertson; Herb Titus, former dean of Robertson's Regent University School of Public Policy; Paul Crouch, founder of TBN, the Christian TV network that is now the largest single broadcast network in the world; former Nixon Watergate henchman Charles Colson, now a born-again Christian who once said he would "walk over his grandmother" for his boss; infamous right-wing bigot and former Presidential candidate Gary L. Bauer; the late religious extremist Francis Schaeffer; Tim LaHaye, author of the best-selling Christian Apocalypse "Left Behind" novels; and Michael Ledeen, a crafty Neocon theorist who first achieved notoriety as Oliver North's partner in crime during the Iran-Contra affair.

The Dominionists even have a man inside the Bush White House. His name is Timothy Goeglein. Billed as Karl Rove's right-hand man by *The New York Times* last June, Goeglein's prime responsibility is coordination and communication between Dominionist leaders and the Oval Office. He has hosted meetings in the White House, according to participants, where "Biblical interpretation" of U.S. foreign policy were discussed, most notably with regard to the "two-state" solution of the Israeli-Palestinian crisis, which Dominionists fervently oppose.

Chapter 24

The Meek Shall Not Inherit the Earth

D ominionism started," Katherine Yurica reported on her web site, "with the Gospels and turned the concept of the invisible and spiritual 'Kingdom of God' into a literal political empire that could be taken by force, starting with the United States of America. Discarding the original message of Jesus and forgetting that Jesus said, 'My kingdom is not of this world,' the framers of Dominionism boldly presented a Gospel whose purpose was to inspire Christians to enter politics and execute world domination so that Jesus could return to an earth prepared for his earthly rule by his faithful 'regents.' "

In order to accomplish their mission within the present generation, Yurica explained, they have a multi-step program for achieving their self-appointed "dominion."

Step 1 is control of Congress. With powerful Dominionists such as House Majority Leader Tom DeLay and Florida Senator Bill Nelson, a Democrat, already in positions of extraordinary influence, it is difficult to argue that they are not well on their way to that goal.

Step 2 is to "weaken the judiciary and revamp the balance of powers," Yurica observed. Using the procedural trick of "recess appointments" to name right-wing judges to office without opposition, George W. Bush has accomplished "the most radical departure from the Republic's system of checks and balances since the founding of our nation."

Step 3 is to increase the power of the Presidency. After that, Yurica noted, comes the vitally important step of "domestic morality and control." In the eyes of Pat Robertson, Tim LaHaye, DeLay, and their like-minded supporters, the imposition – by force if necessary – of "Biblical law" is critical to their dream of "heaven on earth." In the meantime, Yurica reported, Robertson, LaHaye, and their "Christian" co-conspirators want to impose their extremist views of "Social Darwinism, which largely ignores the plight of the weakest and poorest members of our society."

Apparently, the Dominionists have forgotten that Jesus Himself said, "The meek shall inherit the earth" and declared that compassion for the poor and persecuted should be the root of all good works in God's name.

The final step in the Dominionist plan, Yurica explained, is "moral leadership," to be wielded like a medieval battle axe against "evildoers" – foreign or domestic – who oppose the sweeping Dominionist agenda.

While Yurica has examined that agenda, another respected independent journalist, Maureen Farrell, has analyzed its infrastructure.

The first entity is the Council for National Policy (CNP), "deemed by ABC News as 'the most powerful conservative group you've never heard of,' " Farrell has reported on the alternative-media web site *Buzzflash.com*. Co-founded by LaHaye, himself a former head of the Moral Majority, CNP's members have included U.S. Attorney General John Ashcroft; former Reagan Attorney General Ed Meese; right-wing zealot-propagandist Ralph Reed, now head of the Christian Coalition; Muslim-slandering "Christian pastor"

Jerry Falwell; *National Review* editor Rich Lowry; and convicted Iran-Contra felon Oliver North, now an Iraq war commentator for Fox News.

Why should "we the people" care about these individuals and their obscure alliance?

"Bush is endorsing [legislation] which could change the country forever," Farrell pointed out in her *Buzzflash* article last spring. "As one Republican lawyer told [conservative columnist] Andrew Sullivan, '[With one piece of legislation], the religious right could wipe out access to birth control, abortion, and even non-procreative sex [as Senator Rick Santorum so eagerly wants to do]. This debate isn't only about federalism, it's about the reversal of 200 years of liberal democracy that respects individuals.' "

The little-known pending legislation is called the Constitution Restoration Act of 2004.

The next pillar of Dominionism, as chronicled by Farrell, is the Christian Coalition, a formidable force in American politics since its inception. "On December 24, 2001," Farrell noted, "the *Washington Post* featured an article entitled 'Religious Right Finds Its Center in Oval Office: Bush Emerges as Movement's Leader After Robertson Leaves Christian Coalition,' in which reporter Dana Milbank explained exactly how significant the Supreme Court's selection of George W. Bush was. 'For the first time since religious conservatives became a modern political movement, the President of the United States has become the movement's de facto leader,' Milbank wrote." Farrell also quoted former Christian Coalition chief Ralph Reed: "[God] knew George Bush had the ability to lead in this compelling way."

Given the President's religious revelations to the Post's Bob Woodward for his spring 2004 book, *Plan of Attack* (Simon & Schuster), Farrell maintained it is also important to remember statements from Woodward's prior book, *Bush at War* (Simon & Schuster, 2002): "The President was casting his mission and that of the country in the grand vision of

God's Master Plan, wherein Bush promised ... 'to export death and violence to the four corners of the earth in defense of this great country and rid the world of evil.' "

In TV interviews to promote his new book last spring, Woodward – half of the legendary 1970s *Washington Post* team that helped bring down Richard Nixon – said that he had never in his long career seen a President with the kind of moral certainty and "lack of any doubt" that George W. Bush has embodied. In light of Bush's disastrous "certainty" about Iraq and the War on Terror, one can only wonder about the source of such confidence.

Chapter 25

Machiavelli vs. Christ:
A Neocon Bait-and-Switch

T he next major force behind the Dominionist movement, according to Maureen Farrell, is Christian Zionism. Put simply, Christian Zionists believe that the way to bring Jesus back to rule "heaven on earth" is to help provoke Armageddon – and the annihilation of Jews and Muslims – in the Middle East by fulfilling Bible prophecies about Israel. Farrell has noted the fact that among the high priests of such doctrine is none other than Tim LaHaye, creator of the "Left Behind" novels in which millions of "Christians" have taken such apocalyptic joy.

Farrell pointed out the perversion of genuine Christianity and exposed Dominionism's moral proximity to the Spanish Inquisition and the burning of heretics at the stake. "Almost any anti-abortion stance seems nuanced," she wrote, "when compared with Gary North's advocacy of public execution, not just for women who undergo abortions but for those who advised them to do so." By comparison, Farrell observed, the advocacy by Dominionists such as Gary L. Bauer that gays merely be imprisoned seems humane.

So out of touch is Dominionism with any real sense of Christ's teachings, or any sane standard for public policy, that even followers of Muslim-antagonist Jerry Falwell have fled the doctrine in horror. True Christians are beginning to sense that Dominionism has little to do with God, righteousness, or anything holy. Instead, it emanates from the teachings and writings of diabolical Italian political theorist Niccolo Machiavelli, an admitted hero of White House political adviser Karl Rove. More precisely, it is Machiavellianism as interpreted by the late Leo Strauss, father of the Neocon movement.

A Jewish scholar who escaped Nazi Germany only to become a right-wing icon in his adopted homeland, Strauss taught his version of political science at the University of Chicago. During his career, Strauss made observations such as, "An educated elite could rule through deception." His students and disciples have included an amazing array of Bush administration power players including Deputy Secretary of Defense Paul Wolfowitz, Under Secretary of Defense Douglas Feith, former chairman of the Defense Policy Board Richard Perle, and I. Lewis "Scooter" Libby, chief of staff to Vice President Dick Cheney.

All of these Strauss sycophants were signatories to the Project for the New American Century's hegemonic "Statement of Principles."

To help demonstrate just how inherently cynical and calculating Strauss and the Neocons are, Katherine Yurica referenced an important 1999 book, *Leo Strauss and the American Right*, by Shadia Drury (Palgrave Macmillan). Strauss's reputation, according to Drury, rests in large part on his view that "a real philosopher must communicate quietly, subtly, and secretly to the few who are fit to receive his message." Strauss argued that secrecy is necessary to avoid "persecution." It is, in fact, for precisely that reason that the Bush administration has been characterized as one of the most secretive in U.S. history, according to Presidential historians and veteran White House journalists such as ex-UPI legend Helen Thomas.

Such secrecy is no accident. It is an article of Straussian faith. But it is by no means the most troubling or startling of his views. "First," Yurica summarized from Drury's book, "Strauss believed that a leader had to perpetually deceive the citizens he ruled. Second, those who lead must understand there is no morality, there is only the right of the superior to rule the inferior. Third … religion is 'the glue that holds society together.' It is a handle by which the ruler can manipulate the masses. Any religion will do. Strauss is indifferent to them all. Fourth, 'secular society … is the worst possible thing,' because it leads to individualism, liberalism, and relativism, all of which encourage dissent and rebellion. As Drury sums it up: 'You want a crowd that you can manipulate like putty.' Fifth, Strauss thinks that a political order can be stable only if it is united by an external threat; and following Machiavelli, he maintains that if no external threat exists, then one has to be manufactured."

Today, Yurica explained, Bush and the Strauss-inspired Neocon-Dominionists find enemies and evildoers everywhere. "There's a foul wind in the air," she wrote. "America stinks of open hatred, arrogance, greed, and a lust for power. There's a smug complacency brought about, no doubt by a sense of personal comfort, that deludes millions into thinking that because they belong to the 'in' group, hellish results will be visited only upon another class of Americans. So they live without protest, watching the Republican Party become the instrument of the religious right, letting freedoms be torn away from the cloth, the very fabric of our country, and they say nothing. They will endure any hardship so long as they do not have to take a stand against the violent and corrupt among us. Satisfied with the twists and turns this country has made in the last two years, the fiddlers fiddle, while America burns its resources, its dollars, its credibility, its young men and women, and the very heart of our Constitution."

Yurica also carefully established the fact that a right-wing minority now wields, in the name of God, de facto control over the rest of the U.S. population – without the "average American" even knowing it.

At the center of the circle of power, meanwhile, is a man you have probably never even heard of: LaHaye, the multi-millionaire author of the "Left Behind" novels, which have sold more than 60 million copies. In a January 28, 2004, cover story in *Rolling Stone*, entitled "Reverend Doomsday," journalist Robert Dreyfuss revealed that LaHaye is "one of the most influential leaders of the Christian right, and a man who played a quiet but pivotal role in putting George W. Bush in the White House … It's doubtful that such a fanatic believer has ever had such a direct pipeline to the White House."

LaHaye and his followers want to, in effect, re-establish Old Testament law – that of crimes against God and His wrathful punishment in return – just as the Taliban did in Afghanistan. Radical Islamic fundamentalists are said to want to return civilization to the 7th century. Christian Dominionists want to return it to the Garden of Eden – after a holocaust has erased everyone but them from the planet.

Chapter 26
"Poor Ignorant Barbarians in Babylon"

Anyone who doubts the severe and imminent implications of the secret initiative undertaken by the Dominionists should consider a pending piece of Congressional legislation known as the Constitution Restoration Act of 2004, created by minions of Pat Robertson and introduced last February by the televangelist's extremist allies in Congress, led by Republican Representative Robert Aderholt of Alabama.

The Constitution Restoration Act, as speciously misnamed as "The Patriot Act" in terms of its real social consequences, is now quietly working its way through the U.S. Congress, without media coverage or public debate. In June 2004, a press spokesman for Representative Aderholt expressed the Congressman's "confidence" that the bill would become law. Most recently it has been referred to the House Subcommittee on the Constitution after initial review by the House Committee on the Judiciary.

The co-sponsors of the House version (HR-3799) are Republicans Spencer Bachus (AL), Robert Cramer (AL),

Terry Everett (AL), Jack Kingston (GA), Mike Pence (IN), Joseph Pitts (PA), and Mike Rogers (AL).

It is no coincidence that five of the bill's eight sponsors in the House, and its Senate sponsor, Republican Richard Shelby, are from Alabama. The bill is the brainchild of former Alabama Supreme Court Chief Justice Roy Moore, who was removed from office by the courts for his refusal to remove the Ten Commandments from a public building. In fact, the bill was drafted by Moore's attorney Herb Titus, the first dean of Pat Robertson's School of Public Policy and a committed Dominionist.

Co-sponsors of the Senate version of the bill are Republicans Wayne Allard (CO), Jim Inhofe (OK), Sam Brownback (KS), and Lindsey Graham (SC), as well as Democrat Zell Miller (GA).

Although the bill has been ignored by the corporate media, it has prompted reactionary reportage and commentary online and swooning support in the Christian press.

"It is the most important legislation in the last 50 years," wrote Pensacola, Florida-based right-wing zealot and talk radio host Chuck Baldwin, who is also running as the Vice Presidential candidate of the ultra-conservative Constitution party in this year's election. "For all practical purposes, America is now controlled by a tyrannical oligarchy of federal judges ... Accordingly, under Section 102 of this bill, 'Notwithstanding any other provision of this chapter, the Supreme Court shall not have jurisdiction to review, by appeal, writ of certiorari, or otherwise, any matter to the extent that relief is sought against an element of federal, state, or local government, or against an officer of federal, state, or local government (whether or not acting in official personal capacity), by reason of that element's or officer's acknowledgment of God as the sovereign source of law, liberty, or government.'

"This means," Baldwin continued, "that the federal judiciary would be prohibited from interfering with any expression of religious faith by any elected local, state, or federal official. In other words, federal judges could not prevent the Ten Commandments from being displayed in public buildings or Nativity Scenes from appearing on courthouse lawns or 'under God' from being recited in the Pledge of Allegiance or prayers being spoken in public schools."

Anti-Dominionist journalist Katherine Yurica has taken a different view of the bill's importance. "Although the claim by its sponsors appears to be that the intention is to prevent the courts from hearing cases involving the Ten Commandments or a Nativity Scene in a public setting from being reviewed," Yurica has observed, "the law is drawn broadly, and expressly includes the acknowledgment of God as the sovereign source of law by an official in his capacity of executing his office. John Giles, Alabama President of the Christian Coalition, said, 'The greatest unbridled abuse by the federal judiciary for over 40 years has been in the area of redefining the acknowledgment of God as the sovereign source of law ... We define this as judicial activism, making law from the bench. These unconstitutional rulings have gone unchecked by other branches of government."

Politically, there are millions of Americans who are not Dominionists or religious zealots who would agree with such an assessment, in general, of federal courts. However, what all Americans must understand, as the Constitution Restoration Act slowly grinds its way through Congressional committees, is that right-wing zealots such as Phyllis Schafly have already expressed enthusiasm for the bill because it can ultimately be used to prevent same-sex marriage, condemn homosexuals and lesbians to civil punishment, and roll back a woman's right to choose abortion under *Roe v. Wade.*

In a March 2004 *Moscow Times* article that has been widely reproduced online, journalist Chris Floyd offered a succinct analysis of the social implications and political context of the Constitution Restoration Act. "One of the sticking points in crafting the just signed interim constitution of the Pentagon cash cow formerly known as Iraq," Floyd wrote, "was the question of acknowledging Islam as the fundamental source of law. After much wrangling, a fudge was worked out that cites the Koran as a fundamental source of legal authority, with the proviso that no law can be passed that conflicts with Islam.

"We in the enlightened West," he observed, "smile at such theocratic quibbling, of course: Imagine, national leaders insisting that a modern state be governed solely by divine authority! Governments guaranteeing the right of religious extremists to impose their views on society! What next – debates about how many angels can dance on the head of a pin? Oh, those poor, ignorant barbarians in Babylon!"

Floyd then cautioned his readers that "the Constitution Restoration Act of 2004 is no joke ... If enacted, it will effectively transform the American republic into a theocracy, where the arbitrary dictates of a 'higher power' – as interpreted by a judge, policeman, bureaucrat, or President – can override the rule of law ... placing the state, the school, the arts and sciences, law, economics, and every other sphere under Christ the King. Or as Attorney General John Ashcroft – the nation's chief law enforcement officer – has often proclaimed: 'America has no king but Jesus!'

"According to Dominionist literature,' Floyd continued, " 'Biblical rule' means execution – preferably by stoning – of homosexuals and other 'revelers in licentiousness'; massive tax cuts for the rich (because 'wealth is a mark of God's favor'); the elimination of government programs to alleviate poverty and sickness (because these depend on 'confiscation of wealth'); and enslavement for debtors. No legal challenges to 'God's order' will be allowed. And because this order is divinely ordained, the 'elect' can use any means necessary to establish it, including deception, subversion, even violence. As Robertson himself adjures the faithful: 'Zealous men force their way in.' "

Floyd then got to the punch line, the law-and-order new reality as envisioned by Dominionists under the Constitution.

Days after the quiet introduction of the bill into both houses of Congress, "General Ralph Eberhart, head of America's first domestic military command, said the regime must now bring the experience learned on foreign battlefields to the 'Homeland' itself, including the integration of police, military, and intelligence forces, 'wide-area surveillance of the United States,' and 'urban warfare tactics,' *GovExec.com* reports."

What does all that mean for "we the people" who are secular citizens regardless of our private religious faiths?

It means that if taken literally – which certainly it should be – the Constitution Restoration Act of 2004 is a one-way ticket back to the Inquisition, or worse. The full dictionary definition of "theocracy" includes "His [God's] laws being interpreted by the ecclesiastical authorities."

"Ecclesiastical" means "of or pertaining to the church or the clergy."

The Constitution Restoration Act is an attempt to establish God – as misinterpreted by fanatical, self-serving men and women who, in fact, blaspheme our Creator – as the de facto "ruler" of the United States of America, and to remove from office by impeachment any U.S. Supreme Court Justice or any federal judge who fails to follow its frighteningly clear premise.

And all the while, the largely secular American public has been kept in the dark by a treasonously silent mass media.

Chapter 27

"The Family": Learning How to Rule the World

I n addition to the Dominionists, there is yet another right-wing sect of which few Americans have either heard or read. Based in Washington and across the Potomac in northern Virginia, a secretive, tight-knit band of self-described Christian patriots wields enormous political influence in the nation's capital and beyond. What gives these leaders of an organization known as "the Fellowship" their exceptional power?

They are all members of the U.S. Congress, and they share the Dominionist agenda.

The group is best known for hosting the National Prayer Breakfast each February with the President of the United States. Also known as "the Family," the group includes Republican U.S. Senators Don Nickles (OK), Charles Grassley (IA), Pete Domenici (NM), John Ensign (NV), James Inhofe (OK) – a sponsor of the Constitution Restoration Act – and Conrad Burns (MT). The "invisible" brotherhood also includes Democratic Senator Bill Nelson (FL).

The House is represented by Republicans Jim DeMint (SC), Frank Wolf (VA), Joseph Pitts (PA), and Zach Wamp (TN), as well as a lone Democrat, Bart Stupak (MI).

Anthony Lappe, a former mainstream journalist who later became a founder and editor of Guerrilla News Network (*www.gnn.tv*), has written, "The Fellowship is one of the most secretive, most powerful religious organizations in the country. Its connections reach to the highest levels of the U.S. government and include ties to the CIA and numerous current and past dictators around the world." In the spirit of Straussian Neocon secrecy, its members, according to Lappe, have "denied owing any allegiance to the group, and several professed ignorance of even the most basic facts about the organization."

Jeffrey Sharlet, editor of another courageous and important alternative journalism web site, Killing the Buddha (*www.killingthebuddha.com*) and co-author of *Killing the Buddha: A Heretic's Bible* (The Free Press, 2004), infiltrated the Fellowship's Arlington, Virginia, mansion, dubbed Ivanwald, then published an eye-opening article in *Harper's* magazine in March 2003.

"I have lived with these men," wrote Sharlet, a half-Jewish New Yorker, "not as a Christian – a term they deride as too narrow for the world they are building in Christ's honor – but as a 'believer.' These powerful 'believers' … populate an 'invisible' association, though its membership has always consisted mostly of public men."

To foster the interests of God on earth, Sharlet reported, "regular prayer groups have met in the Pentagon and at the Department of Defense, and the Family has traditionally fostered strong ties with businessmen in the oil and aerospace industries."

In a December 8, 2003, story in the *Washington Post*, headlined "Northern Virginia Neighbors Up in Arms Over Secretive Enclave," reporter Annie Gowen noted: "In its mission to create global harmony, the Fellowship has for decades quietly brought together third world leaders, disgraced captains of industry, members of Congress, and ambassadors." Among the Fellowship's famous guests, the *Post* revealed, have been Palestinian leader and terrorist Yasser Arafat. In his *Harper's* article, Sharlet reported that other notable colleagues in Christ have included "Brazilian dictator General Costa e Silva ... [Indonesian dictator] General Suharto (whose tally of several hundred thousand 'Communists' killed marks him as one of the century's most murderous dictators) ... Salvadoran General Carlos Eugenios Vides Casanova, convicted by a Florida jury of the torture of thousands ... and Honduran General Gustavo Alvarez Martinez, himself an evangelical minister, who was linked to both the CIA and death squads before his own demise."

The Family's financial backers include, among others, Tom Phillips, former CEO of Big Three arms manufacturer Raytheon. Even more troubling, however, is the "Christian" worldview that the Family forges behind closed doors.

"The Family's leaders," Sharlet established from his three-week infiltration, "consider democracy a manifestation of ungodly pride and 'throwaway religion' in favor of the truths of the Family. Declaring God's covenant with the Jews broken, the group's core members call themselves 'the new chosen.' "

In a Guerrilla News Network interview with Lappe, Sharlet went even further than what he reported in *Harper's*. "The goal [of the Family] is an 'invisible' world organization led by Christ," he said. "The core issue is capitalism and power." Sharlet left no doubt about the clear message he received at Ivanwald: "You guys are here to learn how to rule the world."

Chapter 28

Murder and Beheading in the Name of God

"When a new government of the United States of America has been established under Biblical law, then no citizen will have the right to resist it or rebel against its edicts," Katherine Yurica has written. "In other words, the Declaration of Independence will no longer be applicable to the regency established by the Dominionists. This is how Romans 13, a key verse quoted by Dominionists, reads in the New English Version: 'Every person must submit to the supreme authorities. There is no authority but by act of God, and the existing authorities are instituted by Him; consequently anyone who rebels against authority is resisting a divine institution, and those who so resist have themselves to thank for the punishment they will receive.'

"This section," Yurica cautioned, "if taken literally as fundamentalists are apt to do, appears to prohibit any kind of resistance against the policies of a government, including peaceful protests, petitions, and writings."

Lest anyone reach the conclusion that Yurica is guilty of hyperbole, consider the insightful words of an online reviewer of The Yurica Report named J.A. Bartlett (*www.jabartlett.blogspot.com*): "You may be tempted to believe ... that her argument is overblown and nearly hysterical, because what she is describing sounds almost loony, given our pluralistic traditions. But in the end, your disbelief in the likelihood of her story comes from your ideological location, which is most likely in what [is] called 'the secular center,' which won't accept that there's a culture war going on."

To the Dominionists, who is the enemy? Who is to be held accountable by God for their sins? Based on her 20 years of research, Yurica provided a not-surprising answer: "If 'Secular Humanists are the greatest threat to Christianity the world has ever known,' as theologian Francis Schaeffer claimed, then who are the Humanists? According to Dominionists, humanists are the folks who allow or encourage licentious behavior in America. They are the undisciplined revelers.

"Put all the enemies of the Dominionists together ... into the one single most highly derided and contaminated individual known to man," Yurica observed, "and you will have before you an image of the quintessential 'liberal' – one of those folks who wants to give liberally to the poor and needy, who desires the welfare and happiness of all Americans, who insists on safety regulations for your protection and who desires the preservation of your values – those damnable people are the folks that must be reduced to powerlessness or worse: extinction.

"Take, for instance," Yurica noted, "[talk radio host and Fox News commentator] Sean Hannity's remarks to *Time* magazine, 'You can play golf with liberals, be neighbors with them, go out to dinner. I just don't want them in power.' Or take Ann Coulter's assertions: 'Liberals have a preternatural gift for striking a position on the side of treason,' and 'Whenever the nation is under attack, from within or without, liberals side with the enemy.' "

Despite such rhetoric from right-wing superstars like Hannity and Coulter, perhaps the most outrageous example of right-wing blasphemy derives from lesser-known zealots who place themselves above the law. Yurica cites the example of a radio interview with Pensacola, Florida-based Reverend Donald Spitz, a spokesman for a Virginia-based pro-life group and the radical, violent Army of God. During an interview on ABC-owned KGO Radio in San Francisco, Spitz supported convicted murderer Paul Hill, a Pentecostal minister sentenced to death for the execution-style murder of a doctor and his bodyguard outside an abortion clinic. Spitz had served as Hill's spiritual counselor. "He said Hill died with the conviction he had done the Lord's work," Yurica wrote. "Spitz believed that Hill was completely justified in murdering the physician because, according to him, '26 babies ... were saved by the killing.' "

Such sentiment can never be attributed to any true God, particularly a deity that universal theology teaches is based on "love." But self-righteous vitriol is also nothing new, nor is it limited to the religious right. Infamous Vietnam hawk and former U.S. Secretary of Defense Robert McNamara told documentary filmmaker Errol Morris in the Academy Award-winning 2003 film, *The Fog of War*, that sometimes in order to accomplish good, it is necessary to do evil.

"There is an infection, a religious and political pathology, that has corrupted our churches," Yurica has concluded, somewhat pessimistically. "Those we trusted the most have embraced evil. That knowledge is almost more than we can bear. Who among us will stand in the gap and make up the hedge to save our nation?"

Of all the harsh – and nearly unthinkable, unbelievable – truths that must be faced about the aberration of the American Dream, including its Constitutional right of freedom from religious persecution, perhaps the most horrifically ironic is how religion has been used to pervert truth and pave the way for persecution.

However, the demonizing of "the other side" is not limited to the religious right. If ultimate truth is to be faced and dealt with, it must be noted that the "liberal" left – those who openly promote "alternative" values such as homosexuality, same-sex marriage, a ban on guns, or unfettered access to abortion – are equally as offensive to sincere, honorable Christians, or Second Amendment adherents, as their Neocon brethren in bias are to abortion or gay rights activists. In the names of freedom and self-expression, the liberal left wants to, in effect, overturn western religious and cultural traditions that have been in place for 2,000 years. Given that challenge, the religious right is now willing to fight to the death – quite literally.

The point is that intolerance is intolerance, regardless of which side you're on, and bigotry is bigotry, no matter how politically correct in any given swing of the social pendulum. Even proving to be "right" on any given issue of the day is no justification for intellectual and moral fratricide, for ultimately, there is no right and wrong, there is only individual freedom and the right to choose, in all situations, given all men and women by our Creator. As history has demonstrated, all forms of extremism, regardless of origin, lead to severe consequences. "Judge not, lest you be judged," Jesus said, in a fundamental statement of universal law found in virtually all religious traditions.

To paraphrase Jesus in modern political terms, extremism begets extremism, a universal law being played out in Iraq and elsewhere with beheadings and human horror almost beyond comprehension.

Until "we the people" stop judging and demonizing one another, and come together as human beings – as Earth Day founder John McConnell has preached for more than 50 years – there is no hope of salvation for either side. We will all perish together.

Chapter 29

George W. Bush: Self-Help Methodist or Messianic Calvinist?

I n his 1994 book, *The Theme Is Freedom: Religion, Politics, and the American Tradition* (Regnery), former Los Angeles Times Syndicate columnist M. Stanton Evans, a devout conservative who eloquently espoused an argument for a religious revival in response to the "neo-pagan" leftism of the Clinton era, explained the religious tradition that defined early America. Evans quoted political philosopher Edmund Burke on the essential nature of the upstart colonists and their religious and political zeal at the founding of the U.S.: "Religion, always a principle of energy in this new people, is in no way worn out or impaired; and their mode of professing it is also one main cause of this free spirit," Burke observed. "The religion most prevalent in our northern colonies is a refinement on the principles of resistance; it is the dissidence of dissent, and the Protestantism of the Protestant religion. This religion, under a variety of denominations agreeing with each other in nothing but in the communion of the spirit of liberty, is predominant."

In the "culture war" of the 21st century, both domestic and foreign, the importance – and rhetorical irony – of Burke's analysis cannot be overstated. Despite all the religious infighting of the time, America's earliest settlers agreed that the greater good was "the spirit of liberty."

Today, right-wing fanatics like Pat Robertson want to take away civil liberty because they disagree with how tens of millions of "we the people" utilize it. Meanwhile, ultra-liberal "intellectuals" on the far left refuse to acknowledge their complicity in the bitter social backlash facing America from three decades of worsening social decadence.

Our country's founders were of a different view.

"The 'dissidence of dissent' was an apt description of these people," wrote Evans, former director of the National Journalism Center. "They were supporters of the Puritan and parliamentary cause, which implied belief in a law above the state and opposition to the unchecked power of kings, especially in questions of religion."

He also noted the contradiction in such a view, given historical circumstances at the time. "That zealous Puritans should have created a society that somehow became the world's premier exemplar of personal freedom" is, to Stanton, a sort of supreme irony. Most important, he noted that Puritans – the extremist Christians of their time, so to speak – "didn't believe in imposing their religious views on others."

Today, the mutually antagonistic views of both sides are being imposed on a fearful majority of Americans caught somewhere in the middle, unsure how to react or what to do. Worse still is the fact that among the most ambitious dissemblers and "Christian" propagandists is none other than the sitting President of the United States, George W. Bush.

On Ellis Island, on the first anniversary of 9/11, Bush "talked about how America stands as a beacon of light to the world, and the light shines in the darkness, and the darkness has not overcome it," Jim Wallis, founder and editor of the respected evangelical Christian magazine *Sojourners*, told PBS in an interview for an April broadcast of *Frontline*. Entitled "The Jesus Factor," the program examined the religious conversion of Bush prior to his ascension to power. "Well," Wallis noted with concern, "that's in the Gospel of John. But the light there is the word of God, and the light of Christ, not the beacon of American freedom ... That's bad theology. It confuses American civil religion and Biblical faith. It confuses church and nation. It confuses God's purposes with the best interests for American foreign policy."

Wallis is even more troubled by the messianic zeal he sees in Bush and his "Christian" followers and enablers. "When one believes that you've been appointed by God for a particular mission in history, you have to be very careful about that, how you speak about that," he told PBS. "Where is the self-reflection in that? Where is the humility in that? Are we asking whether we are being accountable to God's intentions and purposes? Or are we asking for God's blessing on our activities? They're very different things."

Wallis, like many Americans of all faiths, is particularly troubled by the post-9/11 Bush persona and the secular worship of his "Christian" supporters. "I think his role changed dramatically, his notion of himself and his place in history," Wallis said, "and he became Commander-in-Chief of the war on terrorism. The self-help Methodist became now almost a messianic American Calvinist, speaking of the mission of America, and even of his perhaps divine appointment to be President at a time such as this. This raises some deep and unsettling theological questions, I think, whether there's a confusion now in the role of church and nation – the body of Christ, the Christian community, what its role is versus the role of the nation."

Chapter 30

The Eternal Question:
Does God Take Sides?

In the 1960s, as the Vietnam War and U.S. imperialism descended into the sort of anti-Communist messianic madness chronicled by filmmaker Francis Ford Coppola in his masterpiece, *Apocalypse Now*, Bob Dylan wrote one of the angriest, simplest, and most profound songs of his career, "With God On Our Side." Even today, its enduring rage is felt in the souls of Vietnam veterans and the descendants of those young Americans who died in steamy jungles fighting for a lie. Forty years later, God is again being invoked as justification for unjust aggression.

"I think when we are so sure that God is on our side," *Sojourners* editor Jim Wallis told PBS, "and that those who are not with us are against us, or even with the terrorists, that's taking another step. I believe God is in our world, in our history, in our lives, in our choices. To ask what God's calling is for me is a fair question, a necessary question, for any Christian. That's not a problem. But when we place God on our side of things, that we are now ridding the world of evil –

that's very dangerous, that one nation has this role to rid the world of [evil]."

Wallis also criticized the country's willing co-mingling of the alleged interests of God with those of the right-wing militarist war profiteers at the Project for the New American Century. "When Donald Rumsfeld and Paul Wolfowitz and Dick Cheney talk about the necessity of American power and supremacy, military supremacy in the world, as the only way to peace, I understand that as a foreign policy," Wallis says. "I think it's not a wise foreign policy, but I understand it. When President Bush adds God to their formulation and says God's purpose or intention is somehow linked with American military preeminence, that's a very dangerous thing ... That is not only bad foreign policy or presumptuous foreign policy – I would say it's idolatrous foreign policy."

Reverend Rich Lang, pastor at Trinity United Methodist Church in Seattle, agrees with Wallis's assessment. On behalf of Every Church a Peace Church (*www.ecapc.org*), Lang has written, "Martin Luther King understood [the tradition of] sacred American civil religion and was able to wed it brilliantly with the prophetic religious teachings of the Bible ... George W. Bush, on the other hand, also understands this sacred American civic gospel, and has brilliantly merged it with Biblical Holiness and Holy War traditions. These traditions call for the emergence of the Righteous Warrior who will cleanse the land of its impurity."

The problem, Lang pointed out, is that "these traditions are rooted in the personal morality of righteous zeal and obedience." In the case of Bush, the problem is that he has shown his stripes with repeated lying and state subterfuge that have led to the deaths of nearly a thousand Americans and many thousands of innocent Iraqi civilians, as well as growing global mayhem.

By merging righteous zeal with civil obedience 70 years ago, Adolf Hitler nearly succeeded in doing what the Neocon-Dominionist Christians want today in secret:

extermination of Jews and Muslims, except for the handful who accept Jesus in "the final days."

In light of ongoing news reports of abuse and torture of prisoners of war by U.S. and British soldiers, Wallis raises a profoundly important question for any honest American: "What about the evil we have committed, that we are complicit in? The richest nation in this global economic system, in which two billion of God's children are poor [and] live on less than $2 a day?" Looked at honestly and dispassionately in such light, it is easy for any honest person, regardless of religious views, to discern the hypocrisy and falsehood of the "Christian" belief system wielded like a weapon by the religious right.

To anyone of any faith – even to a professed atheist – it is easy to discern the core teachings of Jesus Christ with just a cursory examination of His own words in *The New Testament*. He spoke in simple yet powerful terms that are apparently beyond the grasp of many modern Christians: *Love your neighbor as yourself, Do unto others as you would have them do unto you, Love your enemies, Turn the other cheek*. But most of all, He spoke of humankind's responsibility to the poor, disenfranchised, and downtrodden. "Blessed are the meek," He said in the Sermon on the Mount, "for they shall inherit the earth ... Blessed are the peacemakers, for theirs is the Kingdom of God."

It is on such a Scriptural basis that Wallis is critical of many present-day and self-professed "evangelical" Christians. "It's difficult to understand," he told PBS, "how we [evangelicals] can be Biblical in our politics ... and not care anything for the poor, or not talk about poverty all the time. This is the primary social issue in the Bible – what God says about those who are left out and left behind ... So this isn't for me a social action question. It's not a political question. It is impossible to be an evangelical Christian and ignore the vast teaching of the Bible about poor people."

Chapter 31

A New "Holy Trinity": Bush, Imperialism, and the Bible

Just as alienated young people and disenfranchised old people do in the context of a broader debate over 21st century American culture, Jim Wallis isolates the problem within evangelical Christianity to the obsessive materialism fostered by the relentless "consumerism" and "standard of living" engendered by the Fortune 500. "Too many evangelical Christians," Wallis told *Frontline*, "are like affluent, upper-middle-class suburban dwellers more than they are like those who love and cherish and follow the Bible."

In the Book of Matthew, the writer proclaims: "Wherefore by their fruits ye shall know them." (7:20) Today, when the wealthiest nation on earth, where God is said to rule supreme by the Dominionists, allows millions to live in the streets and millions more to be discarded among the "working poor," Matthew's words serve as a litmus test for spiritual and political integrity.

Instead of the Social Darwinist rhetoric being parroted today as "Christian faith," Wallis proposes a higher yet simpler standard, in the name of Martin Luther King, Jr. "What does the heart of God say about the poverty? What does the heart of God say about what justice in the Middle East would really be? That's what we ought to be raising. That's what it means to be an evangelical."

For his part, back in 1994, under the hammer of secular humanism during the Clinton years, author M. Stanton Evans found equally troubling signs on the horizon in his book, *The Theme is Freedom*. Looked at through the prism of the new "Holy Trinity" in America – George W. Bush in the White House, fanatical imperialists and war profiteers at the Project for the New American Century and the Pentagon, and Bible-thumping "apocalyptic" lunatics in secret sects like Dominionism and the Family – Evans' mid-90s prescience is stunning.

" 'Freedom' in the classical world meant, essentially, participation in the conduct of the state," he observed, "rather than imposing definite limits on its powers ... Under Judaism and Christinaity, all of this was changed. In the Biblical view, the state is no loner divine, and it is not a church; it doesn't absorb the whole of our existence ... The essence of British constitutionalism, the Patriots said, was that no man or group of men was entitled to wield unchecked authority over others."

In a bit of political irony Evans probably could not have foreseen during the liberal secularism of the Clinton era, the author wrote, "Among the institutions that acted as a counterpoise against the power of kings, first and foremost, was the church itself ... 'Had the Christian church not existed,' as Guizot observed, 'the whole world must have been abandoned to purely material force.' "

Today, in troubling and dangerous times, the church – all three of the major world faiths founded on the legacy of the prophet and spiritual patriarch Abraham – has failed miserably to oppose state tyranny and corporate privilege, or defend freedom and human rights. Fortunately, however, there are a few courageous theologians and ministers who are speaking out. Among them, in addition to *Sojourners* editor Jim Wallis and Seattle Methodist minister Rich Lang, is Dr. Joseph Hough, president of Union Theological Seminary in New York City and an ordained clergyman of the United Church of Christ.

In an October 23, 2003, interview with Bill Moyers on his PBS program *Bill Moyers NOW*, Hough took to task all three of the Abrahamic religious faiths for their failure to speak out for the poor and disenfranchised. "It's not just a political pundit issue," Hough noted. "It's not just a think tank issue. It is a deep and profound theological issue. And it has to do with whether we are faithful to the deepest convictions called for by our faith ... The central teaching of Jesus ... from Isaiah 61: 'God has anointed me to preach good news to the poor, deliverance to the captives, freedom to the oppressed, and the year of Jubilee' ... The year of Jubilee was the year when land reform was supposed to take place, debts were to be canceled, slaves freed."

Hough then called on "all of us in the Abrahamic traditions who share this conviction about care for the least fortunate [to] simply make some kind of public declaration that enough is enough ... It is not in the spirit of American democracy to generate inequality, and to contradict equal opportunity in our society. Those are not the norms we've lived by."

With extraordinary Christian integrity and courage, given the political climate of the times, Hough singled out House Majority Leader and Dominionist Tom DeLay – and by extension President George W. Bush, without naming him – by saying: "If Tom DeLay is acting out of his born-again Christian convictions in pushing legislation that disadvantages the poor every time he opens his mouth, I'm not saying he's not a born-again Christian, but as the Lord's humble fruit inspector, it sure looks suspicious to me. And anybody who claims in the name of God they're gonna run over people of other nations, and just willy-nilly, by your own free will, reshape the world in your own image, and claim that you're acting on behalf of God, it sounds a lot like Caesar to me."

Hough, who invested his adult lifetime as dean of the Vanderbilt Divinity School in Tennessee before being called out of retirement to head Union Theological Seminary, then took on, without naming them, the self-proclaimed Dominionists and others who are preaching a "gospel" in direct contravention of the real thing. "I'm getting tired," he told Moyers, "of people claiming they're carrying the banner of my religious tradition when they're doing everything possible to undercut it. And that's what's happening in this country right now. The policies of this country are disadvantaging poor people every day of our lives and every single thing that passes the Congress these days is disadvantaging poor people more."

Meanwhile, as Moyers noted in his introduction of Hough, "America's 400 richest people got richer in the past 12 months, with an aggregate net worth of – brace yourself – $955 billion, up 10 percent from the previous year ... the widest gap between rich and poor since 1929, more than doubling in the last two decades. The Center for Budget and Policy Priorities in Washington has studied after-tax income and found that if you take the 110 million poorest paid Americans, all their income combined is less than the combined income of the richest 2.8 million Americans."

Such has been the social influence of corporate reign combined with the military-industrial complex and its flagrant war profiteering and violent export of "freedom and democracy," blended with toxic right-wing religious zealotry and a complicit corporate media.

Yet through it all, the American people, as a whole, seem to have cared not a whit.

Chapter 32

"Evildoers" as Heirs to Nazis and Communists

W here we used to have antagonism between religious traditions, Catholics versus Protestants versus Jews, now what we have is liberal Protestants linking up with liberal Catholics and liberal Jews against an alliance of conservative Protestants, conservative Catholics, and conservative Jews," Professor John Green of the University of Akron in Ohio told *Time* magazine for its June 21 cover story, "Faith, God, and the Oval Office."

Aside from George W. Bush's relentless demonizing of Islamic fundamentalists as "evildoers," which has, in turn, provoked the vengeful beheadings of American civilians Daniel Pearl, Nicholas Berg, and Paul Johnson, the growing schism among adherents of the three Abrahamic faiths has provided a prototypical model for a Holy War, both on foreign soil and at home.

"For every person who likes the way [Bush] talks about his faith and America, there's another who's repulsed by it," Michael Cromartie, vice president of the Ethics and Public Policy Center in Washington, told *Time*.

Such spiritual divisiveness, the magazine noted, is "in a nation where 19 in 20 people say they believe in God and nearly two thirds call religion very important in their lives." Given such alleged religiosity – exploited by the Machiavellian astuteness of Karl Rove – George W. Bush has cleverly steered any serious religious debate away from himself and onto al Qaeda and the Taliban, along with Iran and North Korea - the remaining two forces in his original, PNAC-inspired "axis of evil."

Bush, according to *Time* writer Nancy Gibbs, "portrays the terrorists as heirs of the Nazis and Communists: totalitarian in vision, cynical by nature, manipulative in their appeal, certainly not devout. They 'couch their language in religious terms. But that doesn't make them religious,' he told a group of religion writers [in May 2004]. '...I think they conveniently use religion to kill.' "

What is most extraordinary about that passage is that it is a perfectly fitting characterization of George W. Bush and the increasingly powerful Dominionist cult to millions of peace-loving Protestants, Catholics, Jews, and Muslims, many of whom see Bush as a destructive force.

Nevertheless, the hunger in the American soul for *genuine* righteousness and morality cannot be denied by either side. "We began to see the upsurge of religious rhetoric in the late 1990s," Green told *Time*. "There was this real sense of moral malaise in the country, among liberals and conservatives alike. They might not be able to agree on the morality, but they all agreed we didn't have enough of it." *Time* noted that "the Colombine shootings, the [Clinton] impeachment battle, the corporate crookery, all piled up and 'led many if not most Americans to conclude that America had lost its moral compass,' says Green."

However, as the corporate-controlled mass media, including *Time*, lent increasing coverage and credibility to the conservative Republican religious right and largely failed to report the reactions of men of God such as Dr. Joseph Hough of Union Theological Seminary, Jim Wallis of

*Sojourner*s, or Reverend Rich Lang of Seattle, the Dominionist movement took hold and now threatens both theology and statecraft as foundations of human society.

In addition to ignoring the voices of Christian reason who have risen against the corporate theocracy and its defamation of the real message of Jesus Christ, *Time* failed to mention even a word about the Dominionist movement or well-informed critics such as Katherine Yurica. Given its far-reaching editorial resources, that can be no accident.

With or without *Time*'s scrutiny, nevertheless, right-wing religious extremism is a serious threat to our survival as a Constitutional republic, where citizens are given protections against both their own government and religious persecution.

"I take the threat very seriously, because the theology *is* the ideology of a growing segment of society," Lang said in an interview for this book. "It transcends the Bush administration. The Dominionist heresy is becoming the dominant theology of the right and the media 'church.' It has a totally encompassing worldview and has built its own institutions. Unfortunately, many government and military folks gravitate to such muscular Christianity as a sacred canopy under which they justify their anti-Christian actions."

Lang said he agrees with Green that the origin of the religious revival on both ends of the political spectrum is based on a shared view that America has lost its moral compass. "People are hungry for coherency," Lang says. However, he notes, the right-wing, militaristic, PNAC-Dominionist movement has become the force that provides such coherency and strength for those who would judge and condemn their adversaries, foreign and domestic.

Despite his criticism of the corporate media as a willing co-conspirator in the subversion of genuine American values, as embodied and recorded by our Founding Fathers, Lang says his primary concern is "for the church itself. As [the church] continues to swing toward fascism, the progressive wing needs to find a resurrected coherency. Progressives have failed to tell 'the big story' in a way that connects with people's fears, insecurities, *and* strengths and assets. The Dominionists are setting the terms of discipleship and with their dominance in the media, the mainline progressive church is in real danger of being totally eclipsed and taken over."

Chapter 33

A "Diabolical, Hell-Conceived Principle of Persecution"

T en years ago, writing as a conservative who foresaw a need for a religious revival, M. Stanton Evans wrote in *The Theme Is Freedom* that "the chief political tradition of the culture is, above all else, a tradition of limited government, in the interest of protecting personal freedom." In an unintentional foreboding of the post-9/11 "American empire" of George W. Bush, Evans declared that "America's Founders did everything they could to stuff the genie of state coercion into the bottle of Constitutional safeguards."

Today, right-wing "Christians" who are, in fact, more like neo-fascists or spiritual totalitarians – from Bush and Cheney to John Ashcroft, Pat Robertson, and Tim LaHaye – are doing all they can to unleash the genie of "moral" and "righteous" rule on the majority of silent and uninformed Americans who do not share their fanatical and apocalyptic views.

Master Nazi propagandist Joseph Goebbels would be proud of them. In fact, journalist and psychologist Renana Brooks noted in a June 24, 2003, article in *The Nation*, entitled

"A Nation of Victims," "Bush is a master at inducing learned helplessness in the electorate. He uses pessimistic language that creates fear and disables people from feeling they can solve their problems." By doing so, Bush and his PNAC-Dominionist ideologues have been able to advance an agenda that is anathema to the ideals of our nation's Founders.

Two years before the Declaration of Independence, James Madison observed, "Ecclesiastical establishments tend to great ignorance and corruption, all of which facilitate the execution of mischievious projects ... That diabolical, hell-conceived principle of persecution rages among some, and to their eternal infamy the clergy can furnish their quota of imps for such a business."

Always brilliant in his brevity, Thomas Paine perhaps said it best in the context of today's Dominionists in *Rights of Man, II*: "Religion is very improperly made a political machine."

In *The Theme Is Freedom*, Evans wrote: "The very definition of a Constitutional system is one in which the governing powers can't change the rules at their discretion." Under Bill Clinton, Evans predicted – albeit in a different political context – what has come to pass a decade later. "The very *idea* of freedom as we have defined it - as the absence of coercion," he observed, has begun to "fade away ... In place of this we are getting once more the pagan view of freedom as inclusion in the circle of power, which is an entirely different matter ... 'An elective despotism,' as Jefferson put it, 'is not the government we fought for.' "

In 2004 America, the ultimate implications of elective despotism must be viewed in light of another point Evans made in his book. It is important to bear in mind that the respected author's sentiments were directed at Clinton liberals, not Neocon Republicans – who, with eerily timed irony and unintended consequences, came to power under former Speaker of the House Newt Gingrich in the same year *The Theme Is Freedom* was published. "Careful students of the modern holocaust," Evans observed, "...trace the rise of the totalitarian movements to the absence of interior guidelines in modern populations, who looked to the state to provide them with criteria for living." He referenced Toqueville, "in an errie passage, foreseeing the rise of 'an immense and tutelary power' which minutely regulated every aspect of existence and reduced its citizens to drone-like status." In other words, Toqueville foresaw the kind of world George Orwell and Aldous Huxley envisioned in their nightmarish allegories of modern man. It is precisely the kind of world Dominionists intend to impose today.

"The resulting symbiosis between powerful state and normless people suggests, once more, the reciprocal nature of inner conviction and outer freedom," Evans noted in strong rebuke of what he called neo-paganism. "Loss of belief goes hand in hand with loss of self-reliance, and thus the rise of statist practice."

Chapter 34

The Yellow Brick Road to "Christian Fascism"

Today, even M. Stanton Evans must feel the spiritual backlash and political irony that have been set in motion under George W. Bush. "In the secularist or materialist view of life, it is imagined that there is such a thing as a political order that is *not* based on religious axioms," Evans correctly observed of leftist, liberal secularists, "and it is this nonreligious order that is allegedly being defended against the intrusion of Christian zealots. In this approach, what supposedly distinguishes a 'religion' is belief in a sovereign, supernatural being. Since secularism either denies such concepts outright, or else forbids them entry to the world of politics, it seems to follow that 'religion' is banished from the civil order.

"This is, however," he noted, "a delusion ... From an earthly standpoint, after all, the significant aspect of religion is the code of beliefs it supplies concerning ultimate questions, about the nature and meaning of the world, and our existence in it. All systems of human thought, and all societies, rest on responses to these questions and have to do so."

Later, Evans blasted extremists on both sides of traditional political debate. "When religious value is denied in the realm of spirit, but reasserted in the secular order, *dominion over every facet of life converges in a single center,*" he wrote [emphasis added]. "The political regime becomes both church and state, and claims authority over faith and conscience. It is this crushing, all-pervasive assertion of power over every aspect of existence, without exception or reserve, that is the truly distinguishing feature of the totalitarian movements."

To his credit, "liberal" evangelical editor Jim Wallis casts blame on both sides of the political spectrum instead of singling out the right-wing Neocon-Dominionists for abuse. "I've said this to Democratic leaders," he told PBS. "They often seem to be clueless about religion or faith, or [are] dismissive or disrespectful. There are religious fundamentalists that we all know of and speak of. There are also secular fundamentalists, people who have a disdain for religion, and many of those voices are in the Democratic Party ... So religious people often feel alienated or disrespected by Democrats ... I believe in the separation of church and state, absolutely. But I don't believe in the separation of public life from ... our basic values."

Today, in the name of defending our own subjectively defined and ill-informed interpretations of our unique historic freedoms, without respecting the beliefs and traditions on which they are based, "we the people" – the vast, silent majority – are on the verge of losing them to fanatics, on *both* extremes of the issues of the day, who have co-opted truth and even "the word of God" itself to self-serving ends.

In the unprecedented divisiveness of 2004 – rivaled only by 1968, the year that America almost came apart in a different kind of "revolution" – it no longer matters whether abortion is right or wrong, or whether gay marriage should be allowed. What matters today is whether the American republic can endure in a way that brings its two extremes together with a common view of what is good and right for *all* Americans. "Political leaders of both parties," Wallis told

PBS in a plea for sanity, "need to respect religious people and their values and the tradition in this country."

Reverend Rich Lang, the outspoken Methodist minister from Seattle, puts it even more starkly. "Whoever controls the interpretation of Scripture will control the future of this nation," he says. "In other words, it's the vision of Pat Robertson or Martin Luther King."

What is at stake, in Lang's opinion?

"If Mr. Bush stays in office," Lang wrote early in 2004, "I think our future will continue to witness shrinking political rights, financial collapse, and endless war. Part of the power and seduction of this administration emerges from its diabolical manipulation of Christian rhetoric ... It is a form of Christianity that is the mirror opposite of what Jesus embodied. It is, indeed, the materialization of the spirit of Antichrist: a perversion of Christian faith and practice."

The reverend also uses a precise term he coined to describe what he sees happening in the name of God: "Christian fascism."

V

The Failure of the Media

Chapter 35

A Free Press: Dissent as the Engine of Democracy

When the Founding Fathers created the modern concepts of representative republicanism and freedom of speech, the two most liberating ideas in human history, they noted repeatedly the unique role of a free and vigorous press. Over and over again, they stressed in their writings and speeches that the critical importance of a press that purveyed every conceivable viewpoint on the issues of the day went directly to the notion of a well-informed electorate. In turn, they further posited a well-informed populace to be the single most important factor in the long-term survival of their fragile ideas for how a Constitutional republic – a nation of laws, not men – might flourish and endure.

"Were it left to me to decide whether we should have a government without newspapers, or newspapers without government, I should not hesitate a moment to prefer the latter," Thomas Jefferson wrote in a January 1787 letter. "No government ought to be without censors," he wrote to George Washington in 1792, "and where the press is free, no one ever will."

In *Dissertation on the Canon and the Feudal Law*, John Adams wrote in 1765, "None of the means of information are more sacred, or have been cherished with more tenderness and care by the settlers of America, than the press."

"To the press alone," James Madison wrote in 1798, "checkered as it is with abuses, the world is indebted for all the triumphs which have been gained by reason and humanity over error and oppression."

In 1731, Benjamin Franklin wrote in *Apology for Printers*: "Printers are educated in the belief that when men differ in opinion, both sides ought equally to have the advantage of being heard by the public; and that when truth and error have fair play, the former is always an overmatch for the latter."

In the era of the 24-hour news cycle and the "fair and balanced reporting" offered up by Fox News, billionaire Rupert Murdoch's right-wing propaganda machine, such sentiments expose Franklin, Madison, Adams, and Jefferson to the ridicule of "postmodern" cynics. Today, any fair-minded observer would agree, the only "triumphs" of the modern media are bottom-line profits and multi-million-dollar salaries for the elite few who are the public faces of so-called public opinion. "Reason and humanity" have given way to gross rating points and corporate consolidation.

Nevertheless, there is a comprehensive record from America's earliest days that demonstrates beyond any challenge that "dissent" – free and vigorous dissent, and dissent on *all* of the issues of the day – was perhaps the single most vital ingredient in the mix of political factors that might lead to the common good for all of the American public.

"The free press clause in the First Amendment to the Constitution was seen as a means to protect dissident political viewpoints, as most newspapers were closely linked to political parties," noted author and media critic Robert McChesney in the 2002 essay collection, *Into the Buzzsaw: Leading Journalists Expose the Myth of a Free Press*. McChesney, author of *Corporate Media and the Threat to Democracy* (Seven Stories Press, 1997) and *The Global Media: The Missionaries of*

Corporate Capitalism (Cassell, 1998) observed that today, although most newspapers, radio stations, and TV broadcasters would claim independent ownership and lack of control by political interests, they are nonetheless functioning in a political, post-9/11, "wartime" environment where there is little, if any, dissent from the "nationalist" cause orchestrated by George W. Bush under a banner of "patriotism."

McChesney also noted that just as it has always been, the press is dominated by wealthy media barons who exert tight control on public opinion, just as did their most infamous predecessors like William Randolph Hearst, who openly promoted fascist regimes under Adolf Hitler and Benito Mussolini prior to World War II.

To make the point that not much has changed in the elitist history of ownership of the U.S. press, McChesney cited Henry Adams, grandson and great-grandson of U.S. Presidents and younger brother of John Quincy Adams: "The press is the hired agent of a moneyed system, set up for no other reason than to tell lies where the interests are concerned." McChesney also invoked Upton Sinclair's 1919 book, *The Brass Check.* "It was widely thought," McChesney explained, "journalism was explicit class propaganda in a war with only one side armed."

Chapter 36

"Elite Armies of Condescension"

T he worsening media climate America faces today began in the 1980s, when "media consolidation" led to corporate news outlets being increasingly controlled by an ever-shrinking number of conglomerate owners. Throughout the 1990s, such quiet consolidation – aided and abetted by Congress and the Federal Communications Commission – accelerated. As a result, in 2004, "we the people" face a crisis of Constitutional proportion: an increasingly less-well-informed electorate that gets its "news" from a few global media barons who essentially control, among themselves and without proper scrutiny, the arena of "public awareness" and political discourse.

In turn, the giant media enterprises are owned by even larger transnational corporations – like General Electric, which owns NBC – and the parent companies have vested interests, from arms manufacturing to nuclear power, that in effect impose a subtle but undeniable form of censorship on their media subsidiaries.

As a result, a media universe of several hundred companies just three decades ago has shrunk to only a handful today. In turn, the American people have witnessed the systemic subversion of "news" and political dissent. Today, wealthy right-wing ideologues like Rupert Murdoch of the News Corporation empire and the fanatical fascist and self-proclaimed "New Messiah" Sun Myung Moon, owner of United Press International (UPI) and *The Washington Times*, control the very foundations of dissent: the information and insight that foster debate as the heartbeat of and rationale for true representative democracy. Instead of getting a wide range of views and opinions, as the Founding Fathers intended, we get a narrowly defined global corporate agenda that threatens the very idea of freedom as Americans have known it for more than 200 years.

In the corporate interest, "news" has been transformed into "infotainment," with the objective not of informing the public but of generating gross rating points, newsstand circulation, TV audience share, and bottom-line profit – all collected amid a spiritually deafening public silence.

Today, Fox News has become a beacon for extremist right-wing political views, at the expense of the more mainstream population. *The New York Times*, once credited as "the world newspaper of record," has become nothing more than a carefully disguised "liberal" facilitator for the global interests of transnational corporate behemoths. Meanwhile, the very freedom and democracy that Jefferson, Madison, and their peers created – and powerful newspapers like the *Times* once defended – stand weakened and withered.

Not only do the "mainstream" corporate media misreport or underreport important issues of the day, but many go unreported altogether. In the era of George W. Bush, when Project for the New American Century and right-wing Neocon-Dominionist zealotry dominate political discourse, such failure endangers America and the world. Today, the corporate-controlled mass media have not only effectively silenced dissent. They have failed to report the fundamental facts of the most important stories of our time – most notably the underlying causes and effects of 9/11, the institutional propaganda employed to rally an ill-informed public to the invasion of Iraq and the "War on Terror," and the undue, apocalyptic influence of religious-militarist fanatics on U.S. policy. In the process, the very essences of a "free and vigorous press" and "open dissent" have been nearly obliterated.

"The mainstream media have a fundamental role in our democratic process, one that is essential to the health of the Republic," observed former CBS newsman Bernard Goldberg in his 2003 book, *Arrogance: Rescuing America from the Media Elite* (Warner Books), the follow-up to his #1 *New York Times* best-seller, *Bias: A CBS Insider Exposes How the Media Distort the News* (Regnery, 2001). "So it is in everyone's interest that they not only survive, but that they also be widely respected."

With media conglomerates showing record profits, their survival is perhaps not an issue. Respect, however, is another matter entirely. Today, as most Americans know, the "news" is simply dumbed-down filler, a necessary evil that comes between commercials. In that sense, the so-called "24-hour news cycle" is among the worst things that ever happened to the country, along with public opinion polls and the TV syndrome known as "talking heads." Instead of making us more well-informed, or more able to dissent, the three pillars of a 21st century Tower of Babel have transformed us into pop culture-deluded idiots. Given the gross incompetence of the corporate-owned mass media to cover difficult, complex, and important stories thoroughly and accurately, the around-the-clock barrage of increasingly unreliable or irrelevant information has led to a sort of mental overload that leaves us frothing at the mouth about the Kobe Bryant rape case or Michael Jackson molestation scandal. At the same time, we are unable to recite even the most basic facts about the war in Iraq, the growing influence of al Qaeda in an ever more dangerous world, the effects of global warming, or the election fraud-inviting technology of electronic voting machines.

But of all the sinister and destructive influences on legitimate "news" – information of sufficient importance that it warrants conversation around the office water cooler or family dinner table – none has been more subversive than the now universal phenomenon of "talking heads." There is, in fact, no longer much "news" at all. It has been replaced by opinions, points of view, doctrine, dogma, over-the-top "infotainment" – all expressed, for lucrative pay, by "experts" who represent one "side" or the other.

As a result, Americans are now so ill-informed and out of touch with reality that in polls and on-camera interviews, they make fools of themselves before the world by suggesting Saddam Hussein had a hand in the attacks of 9/11 or that the disastrous "War on Terror" of George W. Bush has made the nation safer.

Meanwhile, instead of agreeing on a common enemy – misreporting, censorship, and cover-up by the corporate-controlled mass media – "we the people" argue endlessly about whether there is a liberal or conservative bias in the "news" we get.

The sad fact is that there are *both* kinds of bias: a traditionally "liberal" media, long-exemplified by the increasingly conflicted *New York Times*, and a new right-wing media that in just a decade, since the Neocon Revolution of 1994, has fostered fear and virtual silence from its opposition on the information that really matters.

Perhaps unwittingly, as quoted in *Arrogance* by Goldberg, a devout believer in the dying myth of a "liberal" media bias, conservative columnist Andrew Sullivan pilloried both sides when he characterized his favorite whipping boys as "elite armies of condescension."

Meanwhile, the equally respected Robert McChesney, research professor at the Institute of Communications Research at the University of Illinois, sees a decidedly right-wing bias in today's media coverage. "The conservative jihad against 'liberal' media has been a success, as the dominant commercial media present a range of opinion from the center to the right," he wrote in *Into the Buzzsaw*. "One need only look at *The New York Times* coverage of Ralph Nader in the 2000 presidential campaign – his treatment was roughly similar to how *Pravda* regarded [Soviet dissident] Andrei Sakharov in the 1970s – to see how left-wing and radical the news media are."

Chapter 37
Media 101: Nothing but Bad News

D espite polarized arguments about which side the primary bias is on, *Los Angeles Times* media writer David Shaw, also cited by Goldberg in *Arrogance*, sees a different and more dangerous sort of bias. "We're biased in favor of bad news, rather than good news," Shaw wrote in March 2003. "We're biased in favor of conflict rather than harmony. Increasingly, we're biased in favor of sensationalism, scandal, celebrities, and violence, as opposed to serious, insightful coverage of important issues of the day."

Only a lobotomy patient could disagree with Shaw's assessment, regardless of political persuasion. As every honest American knows by now, "we the people" are the victims of relentless and unending bad news. So arrogant are mainstream media news executives that they actually claim there is no market for "good news," what used to be called "human-interest" reporting. In fact, what the media are doing now is diverting our attention from more important matters with "news" that has no real importance at all. At its most malicious, the agenda that underlies present public debate, whether in the press or at church, is even more profoundly troubling. It is an agenda of omission, the removal of society's harshest realities from public awareness.

In *Into the Buzzsaw*, McChesney addresses the cold truth about 21st century American culture. "As economist Lester Thurow notes, [our] peacetime rise in class inequality may well be historically unprecedented," McChesney wrote, "and is one of the main developments of our age. It has tremendously negative implications for our politics, culture, and social fabric, yet it is barely noted in our journalism." To the corporate-controlled mass media, run by billionaire barons and beholden only to the bottom line, the homeless no longer exist; U.S. veterans no longer want for food, shelter, or medical care; single mothers and their children no longer live on the street; racism is a relic of the past. Meanwhile, their shareholders, freed of any guilt that might ensue from knowledge, are happy as clams at the news blackout.

Nevertheless, despite the bubble of moral denial in which media barons reside, there are, across America, in newsrooms large and small, many honorable journalists who are appalled by what they see happening to their trade and their country. But lest they end up on the unemployment line – as did the once-acclaimed contributors to *Into the Buzzsaw* – they do as legendary 19th century American journalist John Swinton noted of his peers: They keep their mouths shut about their honest feelings.

"Perhaps the most striking indication of the collapse of professional journalism," McChesney observed in *Buzzsaw*, "comes from the editors and reporters themselves. As recently as the mid-1980s, professional journalists tended to be defenders of the media status quo ... Today, the thoroughgoing demoralization of journalists is striking and palpable."

A significant portion of the demoralization of journalists and editors with integrity is due to the absurd depths to which public discourse in America has sunk in "the information age." During the run-up to the Iraq invasion –

while well-informed and morally motivated voices of dissent were ignored or ridiculed – the CNN program *Crossfire* had pop princess Britney Spears on to discuss President Bush, who she, of course, supported – ostensibly on behalf of the youth of America. On April 9, 2004, the day after Bob Woodward revealed, in his book *Plan of Attack*, charges of bribery and illegal and secret misappropriation of $700 million from the Afghan war for a still-secret invasion of Iraq, CNN topped itself. Live from Las Vegas, *Crossfire* had on the "legendary entertainer" Wayne Newton to put national affairs in their proper perspective. All the while, CNN's vice president of guest relations, Joy DiBenedetto, steadfastly refused to give any air time to opponents of the war, whose dire predictions about its ultimate consequences have come true in spades. Given the death and destruction wrought by Bush administration lies and mass media duplicity, high-ranking media executives such as DiBenedetto should not just be fired. They should be tried for treason – for undermining the very foundations of the U.S. government, as treason was originally defined in British law.

Even more troubling, however, is the *present* situation in Iraq and the "War on Terror," and the infantile, propagandistic level of "news" and public debate.

Journalist and author Danny Schecter, one of the few heroes in the trenches of the war for truth in the 21st century, has noted the work of Johann Galtung, considered the father of modern Peace Studies. Galtung has identified a canon of 12 characteristics common to the informational asrsenal of modern nationalist aggression. Schecter examined Galtung's work in a July 18, 2001 article, "Covering Violence: How Should Media Handle Conflict?" at *www.mediachannel.org*. Among key tactics for the modern communication of aggression are Manicheanism, which means "portraying one side as good and demonizing the other as evil," and Armageddon, "presenting violence as inevitable, omitting alternatives."

Of all the practitioners of such techniques throughout modern history, none has been more skilled than the Karl Rove-led team of propagandists around George W. Bush. They have been able to conceal the real motive underlying the quest for PNAC's Pax Americana and world domination: the deeply rooted desire of the Dominionists, under the banner of God Himself, to make the worship of global capitalism the new state religion. "A principle familiar to propagandists," acclaimed MIT linguist and author Noam Chomsky has observed, "is that the doctrines to be instilled in the target audience should not be articulated: that would only expose them to reflection, inquiry, and, very likely, ridicule. The proper procedure is to drill them home by constantly presupposing them, so that they become the very condition for discourse."

Long before Chomsky, another, more famous writer explained the point even more simply and directly. "All propaganda," he wrote, "must be so popular and on such an intellectual level, that even the most stupid of those towards whom it is directed will understand it ... Through clever and constant application of propaganda, people can be made to see paradise as hell, and also the other way around, to consider the most wretched sort of life as paradise."

The writer was Adolf Hitler in *Mein Kampf.*

Chapter 38

Helping Bin Laden:
Misreporting the "War on Terror"

Today, as another leader bent on world domination for the ultimate good of his people sways public discourse with considerably weaker oratorical and writing skills than Hitler's, the corporate-controlled media fail daily in their most fundamental role: asking the kind of tough, relentless questions that brought down another would-be Republican king, Richard Nixon. Instead, Britney Spears is asked to comment on her support of the President, and Wayne Newton, a lounge singer, is asked to analyze U.S. policy.

Meanwhile, the White House press corps – which during Nixon's reign included such hard counter-punchers as CBS's Dan Rather, ABC's Sam Donaldson, and UPI's Helen Thomas in their fighting primes – is composed of compliant, overpaid cowards who place their fat paychecks above their civic responsibility.

One perfect example was the White House press conference with Press Secretary Scott McClellan after Bush and Cheney were interviewed by the 9/11 Commission last spring. Several times, McClellan claimed that the President had "cooperated" with the Commission and was "working with" it to get to the truth of 9/11. Not one journalist pointed out in response that, in fact, Bush had opposed the formation of the Commission in the first place, then refused to allow Condoleezza Rice to testify until public and political pressure changed his mind, then withheld vital internal documents and finally even withheld papers from the Clinton administration that had already been approved for release by Bush's predecessor.

An equally profound and dangerous failure of the U.S. media has been its abject failure to identify or report the truth about the "War on Terror" that followed the events of 9/11, or to address the many unanswered questions about the worst terrorist attack in U.S. history.

In late June, however, a potential American hero emerged in the person of "Anonymous" – a nameless, faceless career CIA analyst who is arguably the world's top authority on Osama bin Laden, whom he has studied and hunted for nearly a decade. With the approval of the CIA, Anonymous published a startling book, *Imperial Hubris: Why the West Is Losing the War on Terror* (Brassey's, Inc.) that garnered an exceptional amount of major media coverage, given that it, in effect, characterizes the President of the United States and senior members of his administration as out of touch with reality.

Anonymous – who appeared in silhouette for a flurry of TV interviews – corrected the public record in a way that could, based on his extraordinary expertise and uncanny timing, lead to a moment of reckoning, both for Bush and the U.S. "The message has not been delivered to our senior-most elected officials of the extraordinarily large dimensions of al Qaeda's organization," Anonymous told CNN's national security correspondent David Ensor, "the durability of it in terms of being able to absorb attacks and replace fallen leaders with great rapidity." The longtime bin Laden-al Qaeda analyst made an example of the Saudi al Qaeda cell leader who was killed in a gunfight with Saudi security forces after beheading American Paul Johnson earlier in the month. "Within hours," Anonymous noted, "al Qaeda had announced his successor."

A moment later, Anonymous revealed the truth about why bin Laden and his Muslim followers around the world so despise the U.S.: "We have failed to factor in or appreciate the nature of religion," he observed, "the role religion is playing in this war, and the determination of our enemies to attack us in order to protect their religion."

He then directly contradicted the Bush-Cheney-PNAC mantra that the "evildoers" of al Qaeda want to "destroy our freedoms" and attack us for "our beliefs."

"The primary role of bin Laden is neither to destroy the United States' historic liberties nor our freedoms," Anonymous said with soft-spoken authority. "It's simply to kick us out of the Muslim world, and until we come to grips with that, we are going to be defeated regularly by Osama bin Laden, who is a much more patient opponent and a much more powerful opponent than we've yet recognized."

Chapter 39

"A Dream Come True"
for Bin Laden and the Dominionists

When asked by CNN's David Ensor to put in context Bush's repeated claim that Osama bin Laden hates us for "our freedoms," Anonymous responded: "[Bush] is being ill-served by his senior briefers, his senior bureaucrats. There's no indication in the corpus of bin Laden's work, of his statements, where ... he indicates that he hates us for what we are ... bin Laden hates us for what we *do*, in terms of our foreign policy: our presence on the Arabian peninsula; our support for Muslim tyrannies, from the Atlantic to the Indian Ocean; our support for Russia, China, Uzbekistan, and India, and their efforts to suppress Muslim populations. He's focused the Muslim world on very tangible, visual activities by the United States, and Islamic resentment of those activities is what empowers bin Laden, *not* hatred of our system of government, or our voting, or anything of that nature. I think we make a great mistake by thinking he's some ranting Mullah. He's a very calculating, very specific individual whose genius lies in focusing the Muslim world on actions of the United States."

We also make a mistake by failing to understand why a former pediatrician from one of the wealthiest families in Egypt, Ayman Al-Zawahiri – bin Laden's right-hand man – would become a "terrorist." In fact, according to a 2003 article by journalist Seymour Hersh in *The New Yorker*, Zawahiri joined the fight against America because of the hypocrisy he saw in our long alliance with his native country, one of the most repressive and brutal regimes on earth if you're poor and powerless.

The *real* story of Zawahiri's rage is but one example of the fact that the mainstream U.S. media have consistently refused to investigate and tell the truth about the repercussions of America's long post-Vietnam history of foreign policy blunders and their serious implications for the lives of ordinary citizens in the increasingly dangerous post-9/11 world. Of all the examples, however, none is more serious than the worst U.S. foreign policy mistake since Vietnam, initiated under former President George H.W. Bush: putting American troops on holy Muslim soil, beginning in Saudi Arabia to provide logistical support for the first Gulf War. "For millions of Muslims," Craig Unger wrote in his book, *House of Bush, House of Saud*, "the U.S. presence was a humiliation of Islam that called forth visions of invading Christians and Jews" during the Crusades.

" 'The American government has made the greatest mistake in entering a peninsula that no religion from the non-Muslim states has entered for 14 centuries,' " bin Laden said, as reported by Unger. "He declared that the arrival of U.S. troops constituted a grave and unprecedented threat to Islam, a Crusader attack that marked 'the ascendance of Christian Americans over us and the conquest of our land.' For the first time since the annunciation of the Prophet Muhammad, bin Laden said, the three most sacred places of Islam – Mecca, Medina, and Jerusalem – were 'under the open and covert control of non-Muslims.' "

For that reason and that reason alone, as CIA author Anonymous finally established on the record in his brief cycle of media interviews, Osama bin Laden hates us – and 3,000 people died on 9/11.

The present problem for America is that bin Laden proved to be right about our real motives. A related problem is that the current President Bush followed in his father's footsteps in terms of disastrous foreign policy. Later the same evening that CIA analyst Anonymous appeared on CNN, *NBC Evening News* aired a portion of its interview, in which Anonymous called Bush's invasion of Iraq "a dream come true" for bin Laden. He called Bush's "pre-emptive" attack "an avaricious, premeditated, unprovoked war against a foe who posed no immediate threat."

Meanwhile, on *ABC Evening News,* the network's "military analyst," Anthony Cordesman, parroted the party line about al Qaeda terrorist Abu Musab al-Zarqawi, the man wreaking havoc on Iraq in defense of his Muslim brothers and the secular Iraqis who oppose our occupation. ABC and its Big Media peers, however, have doggedly refused to investigate or report the most important news of our time: that the "War on Terror" and the chaos in Iraq are giving the PNAC-inspired Dominionists *exactly* what they want – a ticket to a Holy War that will bring about "the end of the world," huge war profits, control of oil resources, and the return of Jesus in all His glory.

In that specific sense, "Left Behind" author Tim LaHaye and televangelist Pat Robertson, along with their lesser known Dominionist sycophants, are even more dangerous – and fanatical – than bin Laden, Zawahiri, and al-Zarqawi.

To anyone who carefully and honestly analyzes simple facts, the framework for a long, bloody "World War III" and "Armageddon" is at hand. Meanwhile, thanks to the corporate media accomplices at ABC News and *The New York Times,* "we the people" are kept in the dark.

Chapter 40

Journalism's Role in a
"Dirty and Dangerous World"

W hat's the bottom line on "postmodern" media reality and the best interests of "we the people" as a well-informed electorate?

"The press is in deep, deep trouble," *Washington Post* media critic Howard Kurtz observed more than a decade ago in his book *Media Circus: The Trouble with America's Newspapers* (Random House, 1993). Long before the media crisis reached its present proportions, Kurtz offered a simple solution that has gone unheeded in corporate media newsrooms: "We need to spend more time thinking about our shortcomings rather than chasing after the next fire truck." In his introduction, Kurtz cited a bigger problem than fire truck-chasing: "the incestuous interplay between press and government at the highest levels of power. It is here, in covering the military, the White House, and Presidential politics, that journalism makes its most indelible mark – or, as is increasingly the case, is molded and manipulated by powerful and seductive forces."

In 1993, not even Kurtz could have imagined how prescient those words would become in 2004 under George

W. Bush, arguably the most corporate-controlled and secretive President in U.S. history. Nor could he have imagined how chilling the future implications of such media failure would be.

"What journalism is really about – it's to monitor power and the centers of power," Israeli journalist Amira Haas, a hero among Palestinians for her courageous reporting about their plight, told journalist Robert Fisk for his August 26, 2001, profile of her in *The Independent* in the UK.

Just two weeks later, commercial airliners crashed into the World Trade Center and the Pentagon and changed American life – and the journalism trade – forever. Since that time, the U.S. media have failed miserably at doing what Haas has made a celebrated career of: promoting difficult truth, above all else, as the foundation of freedom and human dignity.

Long before 9/11, however, the conglomerate-owned, corporate-controlled U.S. mass media had turned away from such a challenge. In 2004 America, under George W. Bush, Dick Cheney and their right-wing PNAC-Dominionist masters, such abdication of responsibility by a cowardly corporate media seems Orwellian. Given the institutional lies and subterfuge that have piled up over the past four years – a program of official propaganda every bit as expert and effective as that of Nazi genius Joseph Goebbels – "we the people" face an assault on the foundations of our republic.

For those who doubt the clear right-wing Republican agenda that underlies the modern mass media – while the right wing laments a largely mythical "liberal" bias – Fairness and Accuracy in Reporting (FAIR), a media watchdog group, did a careful study of the three major TV network newscasts and found that "92 percent of all U.S. sources interviewed were white, 85 percent were male, and, where party affiliation was identifiable, 75 percent were Republican," as noted by independent journalist Anup Shah.

Meanwhile, even modern media "heroes" have betrayed the trust of the American people and our Founding Fathers.

As far back as 1988, before the news pendulum swung to the far right, the late Katherine Graham, then publisher of the *Washington Post*, proclaimed while speaking at CIA headquarters in Langley, Virginia – as later quoted by David McGowan in his 2000 book, *Derailing Democracy* (Common Courage Press): "We live in a dirty and dangerous world. There are some things the general public does not need to know about and shouldn't. I believe democracy flourishes when the government can take legitimate steps to keep its secrets and when the press can decide whether to print what it knows."

Today, in that spirit, the *Post*, the once-courageous newspaper that brought down Richard Nixon, has officially joined the dark alliance of mainstream media that quietly allows a much more corrupt President to get away with worse crimes against the Constitution.

Meanwhile, in a revised 2000 edition of his 1975 book, *The First Casualty* (Prion Books), Phillip Knightley analyzed propagandistic media coverage of the run-up to wars. Three years before the United States, for the first time in its history, invaded and toppled a sovereign government based on more than 200 institutional lies, Knightley wrote: "The sad truth is that in the new millennium, government propaganda prepares its citizens for war so skillfully that it is quite likely that they do not want the truthful, objective, and balanced reporting that good war correspondents once did their best to provide."

Chapter 41

The New York Times:
All the Lies That Are Fit to Print

O f all the examples that could be given of media malfeasance in the 21st century, perhaps none is more shocking or troubling than the journalistic decline of *The New York Times,* once revered as "the world newspaper of record." To a large extent, it still is, despite its increasingly tarnished record for bias, inaccuracy, cover-up, and outright incompetence.

In the early 1970s, after a pair of scruffy local reporters at the *Washington Post* named Woodward and Bernstein had worked for a year on a long series of stories about Richard Nixon and the Watergate break-in, it was only after *The New York Times* finally got on the story that an outraged public and a reactive Congress, including the President's fellow Republicans, drove Nixon from office in disgrace.

Today, however, in the era of George W. Bush, the *Times* has become largely irrelevant and its anti-Bush editorials and mysteriously inconsistent reporting have no such impact on a readership now increasingly skeptical of its motives or integrity.

Long after the *Times* printed a public *mea culpa* for its fabricated news stories from discredited African-American reporter Jayson Blair, the "world newspaper of record" once again had to apologize in print for even more serious misreporting by one of its Pulitzer Prize-winning stars, Judith Miller. The *Times* and Miller fell victim to fraud by Ahmed Chalabi, the convicted bank swindler and "Iraqi exile" championed by Vice President Cheney and paid $340,000 a month by the U.S. government for his disastrous disinformation before and after the U.S. invasion.

"When the full history of the Iraq war is written," James C. Moore observed in a May 27 article, "Not Fit to Print," at the respected alternative journalism web site *Salon.com*, "one of its most scandalous chapters will be about how American journalists, in particular those at *The New York Times*, so easily allowed themselves to be manipulated by both dubious sources and untrustworthy White House officials into running stories that misled the nation about Saddam Hussein's weapons of mass destruction.

"The *Times*," Moore noted, "finally acknowledged its grave errors in an extraordinary and lengthy editor's note ... The editors conceded what intelligence sources had told me and numerous other reporters: that Pentagon favorite Ahmed Chalabi was feeding bad information to journalists and the White House ... The reporter on many of the flawed stories at issue was Judith Miller, a Pulitzer Prize-winning reporter and authority on the Middle East. The *Times*, insisting that the problem did not lie with any individual journalist, did not mention her name. The paper was presumably trying to take the high road by defending its reporter, but the omission seems peculiar. While her editors must share a large portion of the blame, the pieces ran under Miller's byline. It was Miller who clearly placed far too much credence in unreliable sources, and then credulously used dubious administration officials, to confirm what she was told."

It was not the first time the sanctimoniously self-promoting Miller had been had, nor was it the first time she had printed inaccurate, willful propaganda in the newspaper that still, more than any other, steers global debate on the most vital issues of the day. "*New York Times* reporter Judith Miller has played a key role in promoting both U.S. wars against Iraq," another alternative media web site, *Disinfopedia.org*, reported early this year. "[Before] the first U.S.-led war in the Persian Gulf, Miller co-wrote a book with Laurie Mylroie, titled *Saddam Hussein and the Crisis in the Gulf* (Random House, 1990)."

Unlike other, more mainstream stories that criticized Miller and the *Times*, *Disinfopedia* and other sources provided important background and context for consideration of what might have been the reporter's real motive in misreporting stories that led the U.S. to war on two different occasions. "Miller and [co-author] Mylroie have both been clients of Eleana Benador, whose PR firm has represented many leading pro-war figures that have appeared prominently on television and in other public venues," *Disinfopedia* reported. "Miller played an important role in promoting the [Bush] agenda on Iraq."

Under the best of circumstances, such "promotion" of a war that has cost nearly 1,000 American lives and wreaked havoc on Iraq and the rest of the world via increased terrorism would be a serious conflict of interest for a reporter of Miller's stature. However, other aspects of her role in the more recent Gulf War suggest a violation of basic journalistic ethics. A reporter, by definition, is not supposed to become involved in the stories he or she reports.

Nevertheless, media critic Howard Kurtz revealed in the *Washington Post* last year, "Miller played a highly unusual role in an Army unit assigned to search for dangerous Iraqi weapons, according to U.S. military officials, prompting criticism that the unit was turned into what one official called a 'rogue operation.' More than a half-dozen military officers said that Miller acted as a middleman between the Army unit with which she was embedded and Iraqi National Congress leader Ahmed Chalabi, on one occasion accompanying Army officers to Chalabi's headquarters, where they took custody of Saddam Hussein's son-in-law. She also sat in on the initial debriefing of the son-in-law, these sources say. Since interrogating Iraqis was not the mission of the unit, these officials said, it became a 'Judith Miller team,' in the words of one officer close to the situation."

For a reporter from the "world newspaper of record" to become embroiled in such a personal military adventure, particularly when her source would ultimately be discredited, along with her reporting, is almost unprecedented in the modern history of war coverage. In addition, *Disinfopedia* noted, "The links of Judith Miller with the Pentagon are not new. In 1986, she wrote numerous articles on Libya, thus contributing to a massive disinformation campaign on [Libyan leader] Khadafi which was coordinated by Admiral [John] Poindexter."

If that name is familiar, it is because Poindexter, national security adviser to President Ronald Reagan in his second term, resigned following disclosures of his role in the Iran-Contra scandal. In 1990, a federal court convicted Poindexter on five criminal charges, including conspiracy, obstruction of Congress, and making false statements to Congress, and sentenced him to six months in prison. A federal appeals court later overturned the conviction on a technicality.

Chapter 42

How Judith Miller's Misreporting Led Us to War

O f all the Judith Miller articles in *The New York Times* that either helped create or dutifully supported Bush administration lies and deception about Iraq, none did more damage than her September 2002 story claiming that Saddam Hussein had imported aluminum tubes suitable for making a centrifuge that could enrich uranium for a nuclear bomb. The story "had an enormous impact," James C. Moore reported in his *Salon* article, "one amplified when [National Security Adviser Condoleezza] Rice, Secretary of State Colin Powell, and Vice President Dick Cheney all did appearances on the Sunday morning talk shows, citing the first-rate journalism of the liberal *New York Times*. No single story did more to advance the political cause of the Neoconservatives driving the Bush administration to invade Iraq. But Miller's story was wrong.

"The failures of Miller and the *Times'* reporting on Iraq are far greater sins than those of the paper's disgraced Jayson Blair," Moore wrote. "While the newspaper's management cast Blair into outer darkness after his deceptions, Miller and other reporters who contributed to sending America into a war have been shielded from full scrutiny. The *Times* plays an unequaled role in the national discourse, and when it publishes a front-page piece about aluminum tubes and mushroom clouds, that story very quickly runs away from home to live on its own. The day after Miller's tubes narrative showed up, Andrea Mitchell of NBC News went on national TV to proclaim, 'They were the kind of tubes that could only be used in a centrifuge to make nuclear fuel.' Norah O'Donnell had already told the network's viewers the day before of the 'alarming disclosure,' and *The New York Times* wire service distributed Miller's report to dozens of papers across the landscape. Invariably, they gave it prominence. Sadly, the sons and daughters of America were sent marching off to war wearing the boots of a well-told and widely disseminated lie."

In conclusion, Moore noted, "Russ Baker, who has written critically of Miller for *The Nation*, places profound blame at the feet of the reporter and her paper. 'I am convinced there would not have been a war without Judy Miller,' he said."

Although Miller's misreporting, given its gravity, timing, and political influence, might have been the most egregious in recent memory by a major national newspaper, it is not the only misreporting or editorial misinterpretation from the *Times* to foster outrage. The disinformation the paper disseminates no longer outrages just right-wing Republicans, who have historically cited it as the progenitor of their fabled "liberal" media bias. Today, even left-leaning pundits and cynical journalists, whose badges of honor are besmirched by the editorial shenanigans of their once-sacred "old gray lady," are equally appalled. The newspaper has also provided new ammunition for angry right-wing readers whose sensibilities are offended by its increasingly subversive misreporting.

Among numerous infractions former CBS newsman Bernard Goldberg noted in his book *Arrogance* was a May 14, 2002, column by Maureen Dowd. In a piece on al Qaeda, Dowd suggested that President Bush had said "they're not a problem anymore." Goldberg bluntly corrected her in his book. "The President never said, nor did he remotely mean to suggest, that al Qaeda is 'not a problem anymore,' " Goldberg fumed. "What he was clearly saying … is that those members of al Qaeda *who are either dead or behind bars* [Goldberg's emphasis] are not a problem anymore."

In other words, Dowd had edited Bush's statement to make him look bad. Unfortunately, even to the most rabidly outspoken Bush-hater, such misquoting, out of context, serves no positive purpose in the pursuit of truth. In fact, its dishonest interpretation of the public record lowers the perpetrator to Bush's level.

Goldberg then cited conservative columnist and former *New York Times Magazine* writer Andrew Sullivan, who has dubbed Dowd's work "a willful fabrication." Unlike Jayson Blair, Sullivan has noted, Dowd is still at the *Times* because *her* fabrications are "politically correct," as were Miller's disastrous deceptions.

Meanwhile, Goldberg noted, "There have been reams and reams written lately about what has become of *The New York Times*: columns, lengthy articles, entire books. Bill McGowan's *Coloring the News (How Political Correctness Has Corrupted Journalism)* alone offers numerous examples illustrating the decline of this once-great newspaper, showing how it has moved from once being a 'liberal but fair paper of record,' as one critic described it, to a politically correct parody of its former self." However, Goldberg explained, the important factor is not the internal effects of *Times'* misreporting, or twisting of truth, or even the impact on its influential readers. Its culpability lies in its role as the arbiter of what "lazy news executives" at network and cable news outlets will put on TV that night as the important stories of the day. In that sense, Goldberg suggested, the growing incompetence and editorial chicanery of the *Times* is a fraud against the interests of the American people and the country. "The cult of *The New York Times*," Goldberg wrote sarcastically, "…holds journalists, politicians, and other opinion makers in a Svengali-like trance. If the *Times* says the sun will rise in the west, then by golly it will!"

More important, perhaps, if the *Times* deems something *not* to be news fit to print, the rest of the U.S. media will also be held in its trance. Partly for that reason, and partly in a more general context, Goldberg, like a growing list of critics worldwide, characterized the 21st century manifestation of "the world newspaper of record" as "morally and intellectually corrupt."

Such corruption, however, is not limited to the recent scandals that have discredited former *Times* reporter Jayson Blair and present, if fading, star Judith Miller, or unleashed serious criticisms against op-ed columnist Maureen Dowd. In fact, the public record shows quite clearly that the *Times* has gone out of its way to cover up some of the most important news stories of the last century. Two of them, in particular, should have had a profound effect on U.S. history over the past 70 years, but in its editorial arrogance, the "world newspaper of record" ignored one – for six decades – and grossly misreported the other.

Both editorial deceits – deleted chapters of important U.S. history that have striking relevance to today's headlines – did serious damage to the political fabric of the United States and the world.

Chapter 43

A 60-Year Cover-Up of "Hitler's Angels"

O f all the important stories *The New York Times* – and the rest of the corporate media – has misreported or refused to report, perhaps none, given the present political environment in America, is more important than one that surfaced in the fall of 2003.

Last September, I became the first reporter in U.S. history to see the full spectrum of newly declassified U.S. government documents at the U.S. National Archives and Library of Congress that prove that Prescott Bush, the grandfather of President George W. Bush, and George Herbert Walker, his maternal great-grandfather for whom his father is named, were Nazi traitors to their country. The documents confirmed what had been rumored for decades among European café society and on the Internet. They also showed conclusively that Bush and Walker should have been tried for treason, because their Nazi dealings continued after the U.S. entered World War II.

Instead of exposure and public reckoning, however, the Bush family enjoyed the still-ongoing benefit of one of the most airtight cover-ups in U.S. history – begun by none other than *The New York Times* in late 1944 and continued by its sister newspaper, *The Boston Globe*, in 2001 and to this day.

The first batch of documents that I reviewed and copied on September 17, 2003, merely corroborated what had already been widely reported on the Internet and in relatively obscure – and viciously "discredited" – books such as *George Bush: The Unauthorized Biography* (Executive Intelligence Review, 1991), by Webster Tarpley and Anton Chaitkin. The same basic facts would later be reported again by John Loftus, a former U.S. Justice Department Nazi war crimes investigator, in his book, *The Secret War Against the Jews* (St. Martin's Press, 1994).

However, not a word of the "Bush-Nazi connection" had ever been printed in a "reputable" U.S. newspaper, nor had any journalist ever seen the documents I saw, and copied, on a return trip to the National Archives at the end of September. Those documents, from the U.S. Office of the Alien Property Custodian, U.S. Treasury Department, U.S. Justice Department, and FBI, demonstrate that Bush and Walker, along with their partners, former New York Governor W. Averell Harriman and his younger brother E. Roland Harriman, continued their secret dealings with "enemy nationals" after the U.S. entered the war. The treasonous business activities were conducted via the Wall Street private banking firm Brown Brothers Harriman, at which Bush and the Harrimans were partners.

The government records show that in 1924, German industrialist Fritz Thyssen, a steel and coal baron who financed Hitler's rise to power and engineered the Nazi war machine with his vast resources, retained W. Averell Harriman and Walker, a St. Louis businessman who became the Donald Trump-style "dealmaker" of his time, to set up a U.S. "bank" called Union Banking Corporation (UBC). In fact, UBC, under the prestigious tutelage of Brown Brothers Harriman, served as a complex money-laundering operation for a number of Nazi front businesses, all controlled by Thyssen and his Nazi associates from Switzerland to South

America. The Bush-Harriman brain trust also included future U.S. Secretary of State John Foster Dulles and his brother Allen, a spymaster for the Office of Strategic Services (OSS) until the war ended. Later, he would help create the Central Intelligence Agency. Before the war, John Foster Dulles represented Auschwitz operator and poison-gas maker I.G. Farben via the New York law firm Sullivan and Cromwell, whose clients also included Brown Brothers Harriman.

On July 30, 1942 – eight months after the U.S. had entered the war – *The New York Herald-Tribune* ran a front-page story headlined "Hitler's Angel Has $3 Million in U.S. Bank." The article did not identify Bush, Walker, or the Harrimans as the American principals of UBC, an interconnected network of as many as a dozen Thyssen-controlled businesses. A confidential FBI memo from that period suggested, without naming the Bush and Harriman families, that politically prominent individuals were about to come under official U.S. government scrutiny. Nevertheless, Bush and the Harrimans made no attempts to divest themselves of the financial alliance – clearly illegal under the Trading with the Enemy Act – nor did they challenge the newspaper report that UBC was, in fact, a Nazi front organization in the U.S.

Within three weeks, the U.S. government began seizing the secret Nazi enterprises and "enemy national" assets controlled and managed by Bush and Roland Harriman. By November, five major businesses, ranging from an investment firm to a shipping line that transported Nazi spies to the U.S., had been identified and seized. Over the next nine years, 28 more Bush-Harriman-managed Nazi assets would be expropriated, all under the Trading with the Enemy Act.

The New York Times waited until December 1944 to run a brief story noting that UBC had "received authority to change its principal place of business to 120 Broadway." The *Times* failed to report that UBC had been seized by the U.S. government or that the "new address" was, in fact, the U.S.

Office of the Alien Property Custodian. The story also neglected to mention that the four other UBC-related businesses had been targeted.

Chapter 44

How the Cover-Up Minstrels Played On

Beginning within days of the discovery of the documents, *The New York Times* declined numerous offers of an "exclusive" on the never-before-seen "Bush-Nazi files." They were first offered to *Times* publisher Arthur Ochs Sulzberger, Jr. and, in a detailed voice mail message, compared in journalistic importance to the Pentagon Papers. Sulzberger never returned phone calls, nor did his secretary ever arrange for a conversation. The historic papers were then offered to *Times* Executive Editor Bill Keller, who never returned phone calls or responded to e-mails. After that, the documents were ignored by Jan Battaile, assistant to *Times* Washington bureau chief Philip Taubman – the man promoted to prominence following the Jayson Blair scandal to help shore up the paper's reputation. Bush-Iraq propagandist Judith Miller refused in a telephone conversation to review the documents, and liberal Bush-bashing op-ed columnist Maureen Dowd failed to return numerous phone calls.

The documents were also later declined, in a telephone conversation, by Michael Kranish, the reporter at the New

York Times Company-owned *Boston Globe* who had reported on April 24, 2001, in the second part of a two-part article about Prescott Bush entitled "An American Dynasty": "Prescott Bush was surely aghast at a sensational article *The New York Herald-Tribune* splashed on its front page in July 1942. 'Hitler's Angel Has $3 Million in U.S. Bank,' read the headline above a story reporting that Adolf Hitler's financier had stowed the fortune in Union Banking Corp., possibly to be held for 'Nazi bigwigs.' Bush knew all about the New York bank: He was one of its seven directors. If the Nazi tie became known, it would be a potential embarrassment, Bush and his partners at Brown Brothers Harriman worried, explaining to government regulators that their position was merely an unpaid courtesy for a client. The situation grew more serious when the government seized Union's assets under the Trading with the Enemy Act, the sort of action that could have ruined Bush's political dreams."

Kranish then went on to report: "As it turned out, his involvement wasn't pursued by the press or political opponents during his Senate campaigns a decade later. But the episode may well have been one of the catalysts for a dramatic change in his life ... Just as the Union Banking story broke, Bush volunteered to be chairman of United Service Organizations, putting himself on the national stage for the first time." Kranish's astonishingly naïve explanation that Bush and his partners excused their treason as "an unpaid service for a client" rivals the damage done to the national honor of the U.S. by the misreporting of Miller about Saddam Hussein's weapons of mass destruction.

How?

It became the linchpin for quick dismissal of the Bush-Nazi connection, in collaboration with a fraudulent "biography" of Prescott Bush, rushed into print in early 2003 by a right-wing religious publisher, Rutledge Hill Press of Tennessee. Entitled *Duty, Honor, Country: The Life and Legacy of Prescott Bush*, the "biography" was, in fact, shameless propaganda written by a former *Houston Chronicle* sportswriter and Bush family friend named Mickey Herskowitz. The publisher, after being notified of the discovery of the Bush-Nazi documents, declined to examine them and refused to acknowledge the misreporting, done in the names of Kranish and *The Boston Globe*, in its whitewashed "biography."

The book had been quietly commissioned by former President George Bush – Prescott's loyal son and fellow war profiteer, as had been *his* father, Samuel Bush, in World War I – in response to a brief story, published in March 2003, by the Polish edition of *Newsweek*, owned by the German media giant Axel Springer. That story reported, according to a copyrighted English translation from Scoop Media, that "the Bush family reaped rewards from the forced-labor prisoners in the Auschwitz concentration camp." The story also reported the seizure of the various Bush-Harriman-Thyssen businesses by the U.S. government in 1942. One of Thyssen's key partners, Friedrich Flick – with whom Thyssen built the German Steel Trust that forged much of the Nazi war machine – was convicted at the Nuremberg Trials for the use of slave labor in Nazi death camps.

The U.S. edition of *Newsweek* – whose original owners included W. Averell Harriman, according to his personal papers in the Library of Congress – killed the story. That fact was acknowledged, on the record in a phone conversation last fall, by Michael Isikoff, U.S. *Newsweek's* star reporter, who came to fame and fortune as a result of his wildly scandalous coverage of the Monica Lewinsky affair. Joe Klein, Isikoff's counterpart at *Time*, who came to fame and fortune as the "Anonymous" author of *Primary Colors*, also refused to examine the documents or report the story. "You have no credibility with me," Klein said brusquely before hanging up.

Meanwhile, other major U.S. media outlets – including *USA Today*, *The Wall Street Journal*, *Washington Post*, *Washington Times*, *Los Angeles Times*, *Miami Herald*, ABC News, NBC News, CBS News, Fox News, and CNN – repeatedly refused to investigate the discovery of the documents. *The Christian*

Science Monitor briefly considered reporting the documents, then decided against it.

Perhaps more troubling, and certainly more surprising, not even left-leaning media, "alternative" media outlets, or media watchdog groups would touch the story. The Bush-bashing editor of *The Nation*, Katrina van den Heuvel, and her assistant, Peggy Suttles, both declined to pursue the story after phone conversations and e-mails. Don Hazen, a founder of alt-media online syndicate AlterNet, also refused to report the story.

Even my hometown "alternative weekly," *Miami New Times*, steadfastly ignored my scoop — even though its lead investigative reporter, Tristram Korten, had dubbed me "the scene chronicler" when he used me as a source in a 2001 cover story about a crooked nightlife impresario.

Norman Solomon, director of the Institute for Public Accuracy (IPA) in Washington and a regular op-ed contributor to *The New York Times*, *Wall Street Journal*, *Los Angeles Times*, and *Washington Post*, initially agreed to help get the story out "to the world" — until he discovered that his four bread-and-butter newspapers had all turned down the documents. After that, despite his assurances, he never responded to phone calls or e-mails. Clifford May, a former *New York Times* reporter and now president of the Foundation for the Defense of Democracy in Washington, also refused to help make the documents public. Within two months, May would be a regular guest on CNN, selling Bush administration lies about Iraq.

Later, even the Center for American Progress, a George Soros-funded, liberal think tank in Washington — headed by former Clinton chief of staff John Podesta — would refuse to acknowledge or help expose the Bush-Nazi connection.

Later still, the offices of the highest-ranking TV news executives in the U.S. — NBC News President Neal B. Shapiro, CBS Senior Vice President for News Coverage Marcy McGinnis, ABC News Vice President and Washington bureau chief Robin Sproul, ABC News Vice President for

Legal and News Affairs Barbara Fedida, and Fox News President Roger Ailes – would all refuse to investigate, examine, or even acknowledge the documents on the public airwaves their networks administer – and reap billion-dollar profits from – in the name of "we the people."

In an era when scandals are worth millions of dollars in book, TV, and movie deals, not even *Hustler* publisher Larry Flynt, *The Drudge Report,* or the *National Enquirer* would touch the Bush-Nazi files. Incredibly – given the report by Polish *Newsweek* that the Bush family had profited from slave labor at Auschwitz – even the country's largest and oldest Jewish newspaper, *The Forward,* declined to run the story after its national news editor, Ami Eden, received a copy of the documents. In addition, the Simon Wiesenthal Center and Anti-Defamation League also refused to help break the story, as did the Democratic National Committee and the Presidential campaigns of Howard Dean, Wesley Clark, John Edwards, and John Kerry.

Chapter 45

How an "Ugly" Story Killed the Messenger

The long-rumored story of the "Bush-Nazi connection" was first reported in a "reputable" U.S. newspaper, under my byline, on October 10, 2003. After every major newspaper of record and national news organization in the U.S. refused to report the story, *The New Hampshire Gazette*, founded in 1756 and the oldest newspaper in America, rose to the challenge. The *Gazette* gave Samuel Adams his first byline.

Its present-day editor and publisher is Steven Fowle, a descendant of its founder, Daniel Fowle, who had been jailed for journalistic troublemaking before there was a Constitution. Given the gravity of the story, Fowle asked a respected U.S. historian and author, William Marvel, to confirm my reporting of fact, based on his own examination of the U.S. government documents. Marvel made no corrections to my story.

After virtually the entire U.S. "mainstream" media had refused to acknowledge the lost, and telling, chapter of American history, a handful of alternative media web sites had the courage to publish my stories from *The New*

Hampshire Gazette. Most notable among them were *The Wisdom Fund* (*www.twf.org*), *TakeBackTheMedia.com*, *Buzzflash.com*, *Rense.com*, *DisinfotainmentToday.com*, and *IndyMedia.org.* In turn, hundreds of web sites and blogs around the world republished them. Meanwhile, some of the most sanctimonious of the "alternative media," such as the often-praised *Truthout.org*, declined to do so, showing the limits of the truth they were willing to reveal.

Meanwhile, *The New York Times* and their Big Media co-conspirators in the airtight six-decade cover-up got plenty of help – the Big Fix had already been put in place.

As I reported in my first *Gazette* article, the right-wing, pro-Bush *National Review* had published a September 1, 2003, essay by their White House correspondent Byron York, entitled "Annals of Bush-Hating." The editors of *National Review* came up with a catchy and accusatory subhead, too: "Have you seen what's out there? And do the media care?" In an amazingly well-timed piece of pro-Bush propaganda – six months after publication of the Bush-Auschwitz story in Poland and the phony Prescott Bush "biography," and just 16 days before I would go to the National Archives and prove York and *National Review* traitors to the truth – York wrote: "There are thousands of references, across the vastness of the Internet, linking Bush to Adolf Hitler and the Third Reich. A significant portion of the 'Bush is a Nazi' rhetoric has its origins in the antiwar movement. One antiwar site, TakeBackTheMedia.com, which attracted some attention in the press during the run-up to war in Iraq, features a variety of anti-Bush 'Flash movies.' One, entitled 'Bush is not a Nazi, so stop saying that,' begins with ominous music and the warning: 'The media will not tell you of the Bush family Nazi association.' The movie goes on to accuse the Bushes of first financing the Third Reich – and then coming up with a clever plan to conceal their treason.'"

It is compelling to note that even *National Review* and York acknowledged that *if* the allegations – originally seen by me at TakeBackTheMedia – were indeed true, they would amount to treason, for the simple reason that Bush and the Harrimans funded their Nazi network after the U.S. had entered the war.

Then, however, York delivered his punch line: "Such material will undoubtedly seem crazy to most readers." On September 29 – more than a week after I had offered the documents in a phone call from the National Archives – the *Boston Globe* ran an equally fraudulent column by Cathy Young in which she referred to "Bush-o-phobes on the Internet" who "repeat preposterous claims about the Bush family's alleged Nazi connections." Her column, like York's, was noted in my first *New Hampshire Gazette* article.

None of the principals from either publication ever returned phone calls or responded to e-mails after my articles appeared.

In the meantime, under pressure from its New Hampshire bureau, Associated Press (AP) assigned a now-former reporter from its Washington bureau, Jonathan Salant, to visit the archives and confirm my discovery. On October 17, AP sent a story out worldwide. It appeared, between October 18 and 20, in a handful of major world and U.S. newspapers, or on their web sites, including *Moscow Times*, *Hindustan Times* (India), *Sydney Morning Herald* (Australia), and *The Guardian* (UK). In the U.S., it ran in about 20 outlets, including *Newsday* (New York), *Chicago Sun-Times*, *Atlanta Journal-Constitution*, and *San Francisco Chronicle*.

Ultimately, however, the AP story had the opposite effect of what one might have expected – a major scandal. Badly flawed by misreporting of fact and incorrect inference, in effect, it killed the Bush-Nazi story before it took flight, in terms of "breaking news." The watered-down, apologist AP version reduced the role of Prescott Bush, as had the *Boston Globe* in its 2001 whitewash, to "one of seven directors," while failing to note that according to the documents, Bush and the Harrimans were shareholders in UBC. It also failed to mention that Bush's share was worth $1.5 million when the U.S. government liquidated the assets of UBC in 1951, after his Nazi patron Thyssen died in Argentina. The AP story also reported that Thyssen "broke with the Nazis in 1938 over their persecution of Catholics and Jews, and fled to Switzerland." That conveniently exculpatory observation conflicted with contemporaneous reportage in the 1942 *New York Herald-Tribune* story that Thyssen had been seen "wandering freely" around Europe by "reliable sources."

Most significantly, however, the AP story overlooked the fact that Prescott Bush had been half of UBC's day-to-day management team, along with Roland Harriman, and that Bush and Harriman were fully aware of the source and activity of the Nazi capital accounts. The two men – on behalf of Brown Brothers Harriman – ran the entire web of Thyssen enterprises from a single suite of offices at 39 Broadway. Even more damning to its credibility, the AP account ignored the fact that between 1942 and 1951 the U.S. government seized 33 Bush-Harriman Nazi businesses and client assets. AP inexplicably edited their account down to the lone seizure of UBC in 1942.

To this day, AP Washington bureau chief Sandy Johnson has neither acknowledged nor apologized for the wire service's misreporting.

In November 2003, another acclaimed U.S. historian, Herbert Parmet, Distinguished Professor Emeritus of History at the City University of New York and author of *George Bush: The Life of a Lone Star Yankee* (Scribner, 1997), examined the Bush-Nazi documents and posted an essay at the History News Network web site at George Mason University (*www.hnn.us*): "Buchanan's charges of a Bush-Nazi past are hard to ignore," Parmet wrote. "…His enthusiasm for getting 'at the truth' of all this has been further emboldened by [Nazi war crimes investigator John] Loftus, who has suggested that Prescott Bush 'should have been tried for treason.' "

Loftus had already gone public with the issue and observed to Toby Rodgers of *Clamor* magazine, "It is bad enough that the Bush family helped raise the money for Thyssen to give Hitler his start in the 1920s, but giving aid and comfort to the enemy in time of war is treason. The Bush bank helped the Thyssens make the Nazi steel that killed Allied solders. As bad as financing the Nazi war machine may seem, aiding and abetting the Holocaust was worse. Thyssen's coal mines used Jewish slaves as if they were disposable chemicals. There are six million skeletons in the Thyssen family closet, and a myriad of criminal and historical questions to be answered about the Bush family's complicity."

With regard to Big Media's ongoing refusal to report the story, Parmet quoted *New Hampshire Gazette* editor Steven Fowle: "If it's true, it ought to be said," Fowle declared, "and it's not my fault that it's ugly." Asked to account for the "skittishness" of the major media, Fowle responded that major media outlets "don't have the courage to stick their necks out if it involves challenging power. The only trouble with that is that challenging power is their job."

Parmet concluded that the story deserved wider scrutiny, as did *Washington Post* media critic Howard Kurtz in a November 2003 column item entitled "Swastika Story." Nevertheless, despite the fact that Kurtz is one of the most influential media writers in the country, read in every major news outlet in America and host of CNN's *Reliable Sources*, not one media outlet contacted me to pursue the story.

Chapter 46

"Into the Buzzsaw": Fatal Fights for the Truth

From the few news executives or journalists who even expressed any opinion about why the Bush-Nazi story would get no ink or airtime, the consensus came down that it was "old history" – even though it had never, by definition, been history in the first place. It had, in fact, been expunged from the public record, escaping the attention of even veteran historians and Presidential biographers such as Herbert Parmet.

Unfortunately, both before and since the Bush-Nazi documents were discovered, there have been much bigger stories, much more important stories, that have also gone unreported by the corporate-controlled media. More than a dozen of them – groundbreaking national stories by award-winning investigative journalists and TV news producers – were disclosed in *Into the Buzzsaw*, recounted by journalists who saw their careers abruptly cut short when they attempted, diligently and courageously, to report shocking news that nobody wanted to hear.

"The buzzsaw is what can rip through you when you try to investigate or expose anything this country's large institutions – be they corporate or government – want kept under wraps," wrote Emmy-winning former network TV producer Kristina Borjesson, who edited *Buzzsaw* and contributed a chapter about how her acclaimed career ended prematurely when she uncovered the truth about the crash of TWA Flight 800 in July 1996. "The system fights back with official lies, disinformation, and stonewalling."

A producer for CBS News when destiny inserted her into the TWA 800 story, Borjesson lost her job and came under attack for simply doing what any good reporter does: following facts to a reasonable, honest conclusion. In the case of TWA 800, that meant – in opposition to the U.S. government – facing up to the frightening discovery that an errant U.S. Navy missile, fired during a training exercise, accidentally downed a commercial airliner and killed all 230 passengers. That tentative conclusion, based on scientific analysis of the physical evidence and accounts of eyewitnesses, even gained support from former JFK White House Press Secretary and network news correspondent Pierre Salinger, who announced that he had been provided with documents from French intelligence that confirmed the finding. To Borjesson's dismay, however, CBS News anchor Dan Rather – a "living logo" for the network, in Borjesson's words, and a man she personally admired – immediately discredited Salinger. "Rather told *New York Times* reporter Matthew Purdy, 'I'll never cease to be amazed how a rumor takes off like mildew in a damp basement,' " Borjesson wrote in *Buzzsaw*. There was, Rather suggested, "quite considerable evidence that it didn't happen."

Based on the actual evidence, however, either Rather was misinformed – or he lied. The *Times*, as has been its *modus operandi* ever since, dutifully printed the misstatement of fact, without proper investigation of its own. In fact, investigators had found rocket fuel residue on the downed airplane's seats. When Borjesson later presented the evidence to CBS News, the network declined to report the story. Later, *60 Minutes* also killed it. Not soon after that, Borjesson lost her job, along with the former NYPD officer who had been CBS's law enforcement consultant until he, too, became a fatality of truth the public was not supposed to know.

In the fall of 1997, Borjesson got another shot at the story when ABC News commissioned a multi-segment documentary from filmmaker Oliver Stone. Ultimately, ABC killed the story, too, and *Newsweek* jumped in to affirm the government's official explanation that an explosion in the plane's fuel tank, ignited by a spark, had caused the crash. Once again, *The New York Times* helped bury the truth under a layer of impenetrable official propaganda. CNN did its part, too. The story died.

Borjesson, a celebrated national TV producer before she walked into the buzzsaw, ended up working at a local radio station in New York.

Despite her precipitous fall, however, Borjesson fared better than Pulitzer Prize-winning *San Jose Mercury News* reporter Gary Webb, whose career ended when he landed the biggest scoop of his 19-year career. Webb discovered documentary evidence that the CIA, via the Iran-Contra arms deal, had introduced crack cocaine into the black inner city of Los Angeles and ignited what became a national drug epidemic that devastated the African-American community. Although Webb's editors at the paper – owned by the corporate newspaper chain, Knight-Ridder, whose flagship is *The Miami Herald* – initially approved the three-part story for publication in August 1996, they ran for cover as soon as the CIA and African-American activists came down on them (from different sides of the issue) once it appeared in print.

In turn, just as in Borjesson's case, Webb's media peers – who had once applauded his work and bestowed more than 30 journalism awards on him, including a badly timed 1996 Journalist of the Year Award from the Bay Area Society of Professional Journalists – shoved him into the buzzsaw. In his essay, Webb succinctly described the reaction of the mainstream press to his work: "A revolt by the biggest newspapers in the country, something columnist Alexander

Cockburn would later describe in his book *Whiteout* as 'one of the most venomous and factually inane assaults ... in living memory.' " Webb also provided a "usual suspects" summary of the viciousness directed at him: "When the newspapers of record spoke, they spoke in unison. Between October and November, *The Washington Post*, *New York Times*, and *Los Angeles Times* published lengthy stories about the CIA ... [but] I became the focus of their scrutiny ... The official conclusion reached by all three papers: Much ado about nothing."

Webb ended up as a consultant to the California State Legislature's Joint Audit Committee. Jerry Ceppos, the *Mercury News* editor who first supported, then betrayed, his star reporter, ended up as Vice President of News for Knight-Ridder.

"*The New York Times*," Webb wrote in *Buzzsaw*, "hailed Ceppos for setting a new standard for dealing with 'egregious errors' and splashed his apology on their front page."

It was the first time the *Times* had ever acknowledged Webb's once-applauded articles.

Six years later, Ceppos never returned phone calls when he was offered the Bush-Nazi documents after *The Miami Herald* refused to print them, nor did Tony Ridder, chairman and CEO of the media giant.

Six months after that, the *Times* would make a similar apology for its star reporter, Judith Miller, after her own egregious errors led to the war in Iraq. However, while the *Times* had helped destroy the career and reputation of Webb, it allowed Miller to keep her prestigious post.

Chapter 47

Operation Mockingbird:
The CIA as Media Manipulator

H ow is it possible that the "mainstream" U.S. press –
which for more than 200 years has thrived on scoops
and scandals – could turn a blind eye to some of the
most important news stories in U.S. history? How can
reporters like Judith Miller of *The New York Times* get away
with fostering propaganda that leads the U.S. into a
fraudulent war, while acclaimed journalists like Gary Webb
and his fellow *Into the Buzzsaw* contributors are drummed out
of the trade for telling the truth?

The answer is surprisingly – and disturbingly – simple.

For more than 50 years, the Central Intelligence Agency
has held extraordinary – and little-known – influence over the
U.S. news media, including many of its most prestigious
enterprises, including *The New York Times*, *Washington Post*,
Newsweek, ABC, NBC, CBS, and Associated Press.

Beginning after World War II, "the CIA began a secret
project called Operation Mockingbird, with the intent of
buying influence behind the scenes at major media outlets
and putting reporters on the CIA payroll," independent

journalist Mary Louise wrote in an article entitled "Operation Mockingbird: CIA Media Manipulation" and posted at a number of investigative web sites including *PrisonPlanet.com* and *Disinfopedia.org*. Among those who headed up the secret, subversive program were CIA founder Allen Dulles – brother of Bush-Nazi lawyer and future Secretary of State John Foster Dulles – and late *Washington Post* publisher Philip Graham.

"Journalism is a perfect cover for CIA agents," another alt-media investigative reporter, Steve Kangas, explained in the late 1990s in another excellent online article, entitled "The Origins of the Overclass." The entire article can be read at *http//:home.att.net/~Resurgence/L-overclass.html*. Kangas noted that "people talk freely to journalists, and few think suspiciously of of a journalist aggressively searching for information."

On February 8, 1999, Kangas was found dead in Pittsburgh, an alleged suicide that has emerged as increasingly suspicious given its coincidental timing following his journalistic revelations, which were then attacked by Richard Mellon Scaife's *Pittsburgh Tribune Review*, which proceeded to smear the dead reporter.

The list of "Mockingbird" media assets included at least 25 organizations, according to the 1975 Church Committee of the U.S. Senate. At least 400 journalists would eventually join the CIA payroll. The news outlets included United Press International, Reuters, Hearst Newspapers, Scripps-Howard, Mutual Broadcasting System, Copley News Service, *The Christian Science Monitor, Time, Life, Fortune, The Miami Herald*, and the old *Saturday Evening Post*. The list also included *The New York Herald-Tribune*, which had protected the identities of Prescott Bush, George Herbert Walker, and the Harrimans when the Fritz Thyssen Nazi scandal broke on the paper's front page in July 1942.

However, Kangas reported, "perhaps no newspaper is more important to the CIA than the *Washington Post*. Its location in the nation's capital enables the paper to maintain valuable personal contacts with leading intelligence, political, and business figures ... [The late] owner Philip Graham was a military intelligence officer in World War II, and later became close friends with CIA figures like Allen Dulles." Graham inherited the *Post* by marrying Katherine Johnson, whose father owned it. She later became famous as Katherine Graham, who became publisher after her CIA-asset husband allegedly committed suicide. Staging suicides, it should be noted, has historically been the method used by the CIA to dispose of obsolete or high-risk assets.

Another major U.S. media institution, CBS News, also had historical ties to the CIA and Operation Mockingbird, Kangas and others have reported. "Sig Mickelson was a CIA asset the entire time he was president of CBS News from 1954 to 1961," Kangas noted in his article. "Later he went on to become president of Radio Free Europe and Radio Liberty, two major outlets of CIA propaganda."

William Paley, another American media legend and a future chairman and CEO of CBS, also collaborated with the CIA for many years, according to official investigations.

Why would the early pioneers of the post-World War II "mainstream" media secretly betray the very foundational ethic of journalism – fierce independence? How did it happen?

The answer to that question is simple, too.

It happened as a direct result of the post-World War II capitalist obsession with Communism and the Soviet Union. Beginning just after the war, Kangas and others have reported, an undercover State Department operative named Frank Wisner recruited Philip Graham, a graduate of the Army Intelligence School. He had just become publisher of the *Washington Post*. Under Wisner's supervision, Graham became the secret civilian head of Operation Mockingbird.

Graham believed, according to Kangas, "that the function of the press was more often than not to mobilize consent for the policies of the government." That theory certainly helps to explain Katherine Graham's 1988 comment at CIA headquarters that "there are some things the general public does not need to know about and shouldn't." Such sentiment is, however, the antithesis of what our Founding Fathers believed about open and free government – protected by a vigorously independent press.

Chapter 48

The Watchdogs as "Controlled Opposition"

E ven more shocking, perhaps, than Katherine Graham's personal notion of the importance of state secrecy is how the *Post* – and obscure "local" reporters Bob Woodward and Carl Bernstein – brought down Richard Nixon during the Watergate scandal. Ironically, Mary Louise revealed in her article – information that has also been reported by others – Woodward "gained access to what the CIA was trying to keep from Congress about its program of using journalists at home and abroad, in deliberate propaganda campaigns. It was later revealed that Woodward was a Naval intelligence briefer to the White House and knew many insiders including General Alexander Haig." By turning his attention away from Mockingbird, Woodward got one of the biggest scoops of the 20th century as a gift.

Despite denials by all parties, it has been rumored for three decades that Haig, working in cooperation with CIA officials Cord Meyer and William E. Colby, was "Deep Throat," the still-secret source who guided Woodward and Bernstein to their public destruction of Nixon.

Today, credible sources from the intelligence and journalism communities claim, Judith Miller of *The New York Times* and Woodward, who enjoys extraordinary access to the highest levels of the U.S. government, are CIA assets employed for the sophisticated dissemination of disinformation and propaganda.

In fact, the 21st century manifestation of media control is so insidious that it even affects much of what is called the "alternative" press – including well-known "voices of opposition" such as *The Nation*, AlterNet, and the Institute for Public Accuracy (IPA). Since those three leftist "watchdogs" are all headed by what appear to be virulent Bush bashers – Katrina van den Heuvel, Don Hazen, and Norman Solomon, respectively – any reasonable person must wonder why they would all refuse to report the discovery of the Nazi past of the Bush family and its 60-year cover-up, or aggressively investigate the unanswered questions about 9/11.

Once again, the explanation is disturbingly simple. They are all recipients of "laundered" funding that comes from the CIA, via a shadowy, complex network of "donors." *The Nation*, for example, receives significant financing through a channel that originated with the CIA and its late Reagan-era director, William Casey. Today, it wanders through the Casey-founded Manhattan Institute, to the Fairfield Foundation, to the magazine, according to the investigative web site *QuestionsQuestions.net* and journalist Bob Feldman. Another cash circuit leads from the CIA to the MacArthur Foundation to *The Nation*.

AlterNet and its founder Hazen, meanwhile, have been accused of "ethics problems" by Al Giordano, publisher of *The Narco News Bulletin* (*www.narconews.com*). Like *The Nation* and IPA, AlterNet goes to great lengths to conceal its funding sources, while launching vicious attacks on respected alt-media organizations such as Fairness and Accuracy in Reporting (FAIR), Project Censored, and IndyMedia. Hazen has also "blacklisted" a number of writers, as confirmed by internal AlterNet memoranda. "There is a pattern to Hazen's attacks," Giordano has observed. "...Hazen's naked hostility to investigative journalism."

In yet another example of disinformation and ego-driven "alternative journalism," IPA's self-righteous Norman Solomon attacks others by a standard that should lead to his own exposure as a journalistic fraud. "Solomon has seemed more interested in preventing 9/11 conspiracy researchers and journalists from receiving any [exposure]" than in revealing alt-media links to the CIA, Feldman has reported at *QuestionsQuestions.net*. Much of such linkage, Feldman charges – and documents – can be traced back to the CIA-supported Ford Foundation. Feldman has also reported on the links of *The Nation* to Big Oil, which exposes the hypocrisy of Katrina van den Heuvel and her "anti-Bush" editorial minions.

Michael Ruppert, a courageous and respected investigative journalist and publisher of online journal *From the Wilderness* (*www.fromthewilderness.com*), has reported on the complicity of yet another impostor, David Corn of *The Nation*, in the cover-up of what really happened on 9/11. Corn, like Norman Solomon, has leveraged his prominence to demonize the "conspiracy theorists" – including survivors of a number of 9/11 victims – who are insisting on a full, independent investigation. Corn and Solomon, along with other prestigious "gatekeepers" of the media left, have stubbornly refused to acknowledge that the "official" Bush administration explanation of the events of 9/11 simply does not add up. David Ray Griffin, a renowned theologian and philosopher from California's Claremont School of Theology, published an explosive book, *The New Pearl Harbor*, last spring. With flawless logic and compelling facts, Griffin not only totally destroys the government's 9/11 story, he outlines a stunning prima facie case for foreknowledge, abetment, and complicity at the very top. Yet despite the enormous amount of documented "probable cause" evidence that now exists for such charges, journalists like Solomon and Corn – and "opposition" publications like *The Nation* – have closed ranks with the corporate media to censor or ignore it, and demonize the messengers who are trying to make it public.

How is that possible?

"Judging by the journalism being offered (and not offered) by *Nation* magazine ... IPA ... Alternet, and other recipients of their funding," Feldman concluded his detailed report at *QuestionsQuestions.net*, "the big establishment foundations are successfully sponsoring the kind of 'opposition' that the U.S. ruling elite can tolerate and live with."

A number of alt-media analysts have invoked a new term for news sources such as *The Nation*, AlterNet, and IPA: "controlled opposition." Before you can understand what they report or don't report, these observers say, you must understand their financial lineage and underlying, if subtle, political agenda. Virtually nothing is what it seems in today's media world. These "voices of the opposition" give the appearance of being on the side of the people, but really exist to serve a purpose for their backers. They divert attention away from the real issues, just as the so-called "mainstream" media do, and they can only go so far, lest they bite the hand that feeds them.

Chapter 49

The Media as Public Enemy #1

As Bob Woodward of the *Washington Post* went on to trade on his unprecedented inside knowledge about U.S. Presidential administrations and Washington politics, in a string of best-selling books that made him rich and famous, his former colleague Carl Bernstein went on, ironically, to write about Operation Mockingbird. In an October 1977 article in *Rolling Stone*, Bernstein reported in riveting detail about how the CIA had, in effect, undermined public knowledge and the American people with astonishing sophistication. As a respected journalist who had already proven himself on a story of major historical importance, Bernstein revealed that the sinister influence of spymasters reached into the most important newsrooms in the country.

"Sources told Bernstein that *The New York Times*, America's most respected newspaper at the time, was one of the CIA's closest media collaborators," another alt-media investigative reporter, David Guyatt, wrote in "Subverting the Media," posted at the British web site *DeepBlackLies.co.uk* and a number of other sites, including *Disinfopedia*. "Seeking to spread the blame, *The New York Times* published an article in

December 1977, revealing that 'more than 800 news and public information organizations and individuals' had participated in the CIA's covert subversion of the media."

Bernstein named the most high-level Mockingbird operatives as Katherine Graham of the *Washington Post*, Henry Luce of Time Inc., William Paley of CBS, the Sulzberger family, owners of *The New York Times*, and "publishing magnate" Richard Mellon Scaife, who would, 20 years later, lead the "vast right-wing conspiracy" that went after Bill Clinton with such vengeance.

For the CIA, the practical power of such relationships paid premium dividends. "'One journalist is worth 20 agents,' a high-level source told Bernstein," Guyatt noted in his article. As for the long, tired myth of a "liberal" bias in the news, "The CIA owns everyone of any significance in the major media," former CIA Director William Colby once proclaimed proudly.

The dark influence of such long-standing and thorough infiltration of the mechanism for what James Madison called "popular information" – the knowledge that the populace needs to wield its proper influence as self-governing citizens – cannot be overstated. The fact that *The New York Times*, the most influential newspaper in the world, would sell its soul to the very institutions it was supposed to be a watchdog against in the name of freedom and democracy, is more destructive than the average American can comprehend. Yet, the problem reaches far beyond the *Times*, into the very heartland of America.

"Most consumers of the corporate media were – and are – unaware of the effect that the salting of public opinion has on their own beliefs," Alex Constantine, another alt-media investigative reporter, wrote in 2000 in an online article entitled "Tales from the Crypt." "A network anchorman in time of national crisis is an instrument of psychological warfare in the Mockingbird media." The entire article can be read at *www.alexconstantine.50megs.com/the_cia_and.html*.

To the average American, such "paranoid" rhetoric will seem, at first, to be the stuff of conspiracy theories. It can only be hoped that such skeptics, threatened with the extinction of their rights and freedoms under corporate rule masquerading as democracy, with state-imposed censorship mimicking a free and open press, will take the time to investigate the facts and ample public record.

After the Church Committee of the U.S. Senate exposed the widespread CIA-media connection – largely to a reaction of apathy and silence from the great majority of the American people – the far-right had to find a new avenue for its subversion of public knowledge. It did so via the creation of right-wing "think tanks" such as the Cato Institute, whose original board of directors included none other than right-wing ideologue Rupert Murdoch, one of the most powerful forces in the U.S. media. Another CATO-friendly corporate power, as reported by Steve Kangas, was Viacom and its CEO, Sumner Redstone, yet another former intelligence official from World War II. Today, Viacom owns CBS, a string of TV stations, radio giant Infinity Broadcasting, book publisher Simon & Schuster, and a vast cultural empire that includes MTV.

Other new forces within the right-wing Washington think tank community include *National Review* Washington editor Kate O'Beirne and Murdoch's *The Weekly Standard*, editorial home to PNAC strategist William Kristol. O'Beirne is among the clique of big-name journalists who repeatedly refused to report the Bush-Nazi documents, which clearly discredited the pro-Bush propaganda her magazine had published in its "Annals of Bush-Hating" essay.

As a result of such right-wing influence, the media environment in the U.S. today is so poisoned that even its most influential big names will not risk their careers to defend truth and honor.

In 1974, CBS's Dan Rather stood up, courageously and famously, at a Richard Nixon press conference and informed him the American people needed to know whether the

President of the United States was a "crook," prompting a now-legendary and history-altering response. Last year, Rather told expatriate journalist Greg Palast in a BBC interview that in the post-9/11 political-journalistic climate, reporting such a big, controversial story would be tantamount to hanging a "burning tire" around his neck – a heinous practice that came to be known as "necklacing" in apartheid-era South Africa.

Multi-millionaire "newswoman" Diane Sawyer of ABC admitted to a friend in Miami – celebrity contractor Wallace Tutt, who designed South Beach's Versace mansion for the late fashion mogul – that "when you're making the kind of money we make, you're not going to risk it all for any one particular story" – meaning a scoop that might offend the powers that be, either within the network or at the White House.

In light of the stranglehold giant corporations have on the American media, such cowardice is understandable, Carl Jensen of Project Censored observed in *Into the Buzzsaw*. "It would be a truly naïve journalist at NBC," Jensen observed, "who would expect his network to air a report on the hazards of low-level radiation by nuclear reactors built by General Electric, which owns NBC." As for ABC, Jensen noted, "It doesn't take long for the bright young journalist ... to recognize that the chairman of the board at Disney, which happens to own ABC, does not appreciate aggressive journalists who might be tempted to investigate reported cases of employee discrimination at Disney World. This kind of corporate socialization has been exacerbated by the multi-billion-dollar mega-media mergers that created [the] international giants."

Such practical reality, however, flies in the face of the profoundly important observation made by James Madison long before there was a mass media: "Knowledge will forever govern ignorance, and a people who mean to be their own governors must arm themselves with the power which knowledge gives."

By Madison's standard, "we the people" are presently unfit to govern ourselves.

Chapter 50

War is Peace:
The Perversion of Language and Truth

The press is "extremely centralized, and most of it is owned by wealthy men who have every motive to be dishonest on certain important topics," a man named Eric Arthur Blair, a formerly homeless itinerant laborer who became a journalist in the 1930s, wrote at the end of World War II. "At any given moment there is an orthodoxy, a body of ideas which it is assumed that all right-thinking people will accept without question. It is not exactly forbidden to say this, that, or the other, but it is 'not done' to say it, just as in mid-Victorian times it was 'not done' to mention trousers in the presence of a lady. Anyone who challenges the prevailing orthodoxy finds himself silenced with surprising effectiveness."

Blair then posed the simple, obvious question that cuts to the essence of any notion of free speech and democratic dissent. "Is every opinion, however unpopular – however foolish, even – entitled to a hearing?" he asked. "Now, when one demands liberty of speech and of the press, one is not demanding absolute liberty. There always must be, or at any rate there always will be, some degree of censorship, so long as organized societies endure. But freedom, as Rosa Luxembourg said, is 'freedom for the other fellow.' The same principle is contained in the famous words of Voltaire: 'I detest what you say; I will defend to the death your right to say it.' If the intellectual liberty which without a doubt has been one of the distinguishing marks of western civilization means anything at all, it means that everyone shall have the right to say and to print what he believes to be the truth, provided only that it does not harm the rest of the community in some quite unmistakable way."

Blair then lamented the present state of affairs as the world looked to a post-war political reality still taking shape. "There is now a widespread tendency to argue," he wrote, "that one can only defend democracy by totalitarian methods. If one loves democracy, the argument runs, one must crush its enemies by no matter what means. And who are its enemies? It always appears that they are not only those who attack it openly and consciously, but those who 'objectively' endanger it by spreading mistaken doctrines. In other words, defending democracy involves destroying all independence of thought."

He then issued a warning for future generations: "These people don't see that if you encourage totalitarian methods, the time may come when they will be used against you instead of for you ... Tolerance and decency are deeply rooted ... but they are not indestructible, and they have to be kept alive partly by conscious effort. The result of preaching totalitarian doctrines is to weaken the instinct by means of which free peoples know what is or is not dangerous."

Those words were written by a man who soon would become known to the world, for all posterity, under a different name, a pen name: George Orwell. They are from the introduction, not published in the original edition, to his allegorical novel, *Animal Farm*, published in 1947 and telling "a fairy tale" about Soviet Russia and the iron rule of Joseph Stalin.

In 1946, the same year he authored those words, Orwell wrote, in an essay entitled "Politics and the English Language," a passage that is eerily illuminating of the political rhetoric of George W. Bush and his inner circle: "In our time, political speech and writing are largely the defense of the indefensible. Things like the continuance of British rule in India, the Russian purges and deportations, the dropping of the atom bombs on Japan, can indeed be defended, but only by arguments which are too brutal for most people to face, and which do not square with the professed aims of the political parties. Thus political language has to consist largely of euphemism, question-begging, and sheer cloudy vagueness. Defenseless villages are bombarded from the air, the inhabitants driven out into the countryside, the cattle machine-gunned, the huts set on fire with incendiary bullets: This is called *pacification*. Millions of peasants are robbed of their farms and sent trudging along the roads with no more than they can carry: This is called *transfer of population* or *rectification of frontiers*. People are imprisoned for years without trial, or shot in the back of the neck or sent to die of scurvy in Arctic lumber camps: This is called *elimination of unreliable elements*. Such phraseology is needed if one wants to name things without calling up mental pictures of them."

In the Bush-Cheney-PNAC-Dominionist world of the early 21st century, perhaps not even Orwell could have imagined the extent of the simple-minded yet brilliantly successful perversion of language in the service of propaganda. His elemental notion that in the name of "truth," war could be presented as peace, slavery as freedom, ignorance as strength, has been used today to invert reality to serve the interests of corporate masters "we the people," in our alienation and denial, do not even see as masters. "Postmodern" life has, for many millions of Americans, become a materialistic, soulless nightmare of struggle for survival in a culture of Social Darwinism, where – as Hitler so presciently observed – hell can be seen as heaven.

Chapter 51

Spiritual Weapons as Extinction Weapons

O rwell realized – and revealed – that "language has the power in politics to mask the truth and mislead the public," Canadian essayist Jem Berkes of the University of Manitoba wrote in "Language as the 'Ultimate Weapon' in *1984*" in February 2000 (*http://home.cc.umanitoba.ca/~umberkes/1984_language.html*).

"Orwell shows how language can be used politically to deceive and manipulate people, leading to a society in which the people unquestioningly obey their government and mindlessly accept all propaganda as reality," Berkes observed. "Language becomes a mind-control tool, with the ultimate goal being the destruction of will and imagination."

Berkes invoked yet another Orwell essayist, John Wain, to make the point that the novelist's "vision of *1984* does not include extinction weapons ... He is not interested in extinction weapons because, fundamentally, they do not frighten him as much as spiritual ones." Still another writer, Paul Chilton, is noted for suggesting that "the language theme in Orwell's novel [*1984*] has its roots in the story of the biblical Tower of Babel. When God destroys the Towel of

Babel, the civilizations which have contributed to the construction of the Tower suffer ever-after from the Curse of Confusion. The Curse both makes languages 'mutually unintelligible,' and alters their nature so that 'they no longer lucidly [express] the nature of things, but rather [obscure] and [distort] them.' Orwell's Newspeak, the ultra-political new language introduced in *1984*, does precisely that: It facilitates deception and manipulation, and its purpose is to restrict understanding of the real world.

"Whereas people generally strive to expand their lexicon," Berkes explained, "the government in *1984* actually aims to cut back the Newspeak vocabulary. One of the Newspeak engineers says, '[We're] cutting the language down to the bone ... Newspeak is the only language in the world whose vocabulary gets smaller every year.'

In the lexicon of George W. Bush and his PNAC-Dominionist corporate henchmen, just a few terms – all used to characterize Iraqis defending their country against invasion and Muslims defending their religion against spiritual assault by "Christian" fanatics – are employed: *evildoers, thugs, assassins, barbarians*. At the same time, the term used more than any other – relentlessly, around the clock, by every corporate media outlet, pundit, talking head, and right-wing columnist or commentator – is "Islamic fundamentalist." Nowhere and never is *Christian* fundamentalism mentioned as its even more dangerous counterpart in human hatred and violence. Worse still, in light of the exposure of Bush administration lies that supported the U.S. invasion of Iraq and its disastrous aftermath, the President speaks in reality-inverting sound bites like "the world is a safer place" under his "leadership." Such claims are easily refuted with the corrected U.S. State Department report that shows terrorism-related deaths and injuries nearly tripled in the year following the launch of Bush's "War on Terror."

"By manipulating the language," Berkes observed in his essay, "the government wishes to alter the public's way of thinking. This can be done, psychologists theorize, because the words that are available for the purpose of communicating thought tend to influence the way people think ... The Party is interested in masking the truth, and so the media manipulates language to present a distorted reality. As Orwell says in his essay 'Politics and the English Language,' 'Political language ... is designed to make lies sound truthful and murder respectable.' "

In *1984*, Berkes explains, "The totalitarian state of Oceania is in a constant state of war, and part of the Party's ongoing struggle is to keep the public satisfied with this warfare. If the public were dissatisfied, they would ... possibly rebel against the Party. The Party therefore has to distract the public's attention away from the negative side of warfare, and they use the media to do this. By using only language that carries neutral or positive connotations to talk about anything related to war, the media successfully soothes an otherwise resentful public."

In the specific context of precisely what the mainstream U.S. media have done to support the invasion and occupation of Iraq – in flagrant contravention of the fact that exactly the negative consequences predicted by those opposed to the war beforehand have come true in spades – Berkes' observation is stunning in its power.

"In many ways," he wrote – before George W. Bush was even elected, and more than three years before the Iraq misadventure in Pax Americana – "the media is relying on the principle that a piece of information that is repeated often enough becomes accepted as truth."

Chapter 52

Fooling All the People All of the Time

Given the present climate in the U.S. and the world, with political polarization and lack of communication between the two sides as gaping as they have been since the height of the Cold War in the 1960s, it is somewhat astonishing – and ultimately inspiring – that Orwell's singular voice is being raised again in the debate. Last spring, a documentary film entitled *Orwell Rolls in His Grave*, directed by Robert Kane Pappas, made its debut to silence from the corporate-controlled major media. Dubbed "a marvel of passionate succinctness" by *Variety*, the 95-minute film "critically examines the Fourth Estate, once considered the bastion of American democracy. The movie asks, 'Could a media system – a system controlled by a few global corporations, with the ability to overwhelm all competing voices – be able to turn lies into truth?" Asked the official web site of the Philadelphia Film Festival early in 2004: "Has America entered an Orwellian world of double-speak, where outright lies can pass for the truth?"

A year after the invasion of Iraq and the desecration of America's reputation around the world by the human rights abuses at Abu Ghraib prison and Guantanamo Bay and their cover-up, the answer to that question has become painfully clear.

What is most interesting – and telling – about *Orwell Rolls in His Grave* is that unlike Michael Moore's *Fahrenheit 9/11*, released in late June 2004 to international fanfare and box office records, the more serious and compelling film, *Orwell*, got nowhere near the attention.

Mark Crispin Miller – an NYU media professor interviewed in the film along with Charles Lewis, ex-*60 Minutes* producer and now head of the Center for Public Integrity (CPI) in Washington, and fiercely independent Vermont Congressman and media reformer Bernie Sanders – has explained why. "[Miller] explains in the film," commentator Ron Kaufman wrote in an online review posted at *TurnOffYourTV.com*, "individuals may get headlines and specific companies may be investigated in newspapers and TV, but *the system* will never be scrutinized. Big media will never admit that it has influence over our world and corporations may allow airtime for parts of the truth, but the *whole truth* will never get broadcast."

What might that whole truth be?

It would grow from a central theme of *Animal Farm* and *1984*, among other, less-well-known treatises on fascism: the desire of man to be master of his brethren – in the name of all that is fair, decent, and good.

By no means is it the unique domain of the "evil dictators" of history.

In his article, "Tales from the Crypt," about the CIA's post-World War II media infiltration program, Operation Mockingbird, Alex Constantine quoted Henry Luce – the creator, with *Time*, *Life*, and *Fortune* magazines, of what became the present global giant Time-Warner – from a March 1947 article in *Life*: "World War III has begun," Luce proclaimed. "It is in the opening skirmish stage already." Constantine noted, "The issue featured an excerpt of a book by James Burnham, who called for the creation of an

'American Empire ... world-dominating in political power, set up at least in part through coercion – probably including war, but certainly the threat of war – and in which one group of people would hold more than its equal share of power.'

"George Seldes, the famed anti-fascist media critic," Constantine added, "drew down on Luce in 1947, explaining that 'although avoiding typical Hitlerian phrases, the same doctrine of a superior people taking over the world and ruling it, began to appear in the press, whereas the organs of Wall Street were much more honest in favoring a doctrine inevitably leading to war if it brought greater commercial markets under the American flag."

To the American public of the 21st century, it is, no doubt, still a comfort to think of the Soviet Union as an "evil empire," as the late Ronald Reagan so successfully characterized it. It is probably disquieting to learn that immediately after World War II, the United States – and many of its most prominent and respected voices of public debate – shared the *same goal* of world domination, the goal of all empires throughout human history.

In his *Into the Buzzsaw* essay, Gary Webb – the career reporter who saw his livelihood destroyed when he uncovered the truth of CIA drug trafficking – wrote: "Do we have a free press today? Sure we do. It's free to report all the sex scandals it wants, all the stock market news we can handle, every new health fad that comes down the pike, and every celebrity marriage or divorce that happens. But when it comes to the real down and dirty stuff – stories like Tailwind, the October Surprise, the El Mozote massacre, corporate corruption, or CIA involvement in drug trafficking – that's where we begin to see the limits of our freedom.

"Back in 1938, when fascism was sweeping Europe," Webb concluded, "legendary investigative reporter George Seldes observed, in his book, *The Lords of the Press*, that 'it *is* possible to fool all the people all the time – when government and press cooperate.' Unfortunately, we have reached that point."

VI

Are We Living in a Neo-Fascist State?

Chapter 53

Beyond 1984:
Defining the Other "F" Word

I n the activist-oriented 1960s, the *political* "F" word – fascism – was used with such relentless regularity, and relative historic inaccuracy, that it has been demonized ever since as a term employed almost exclusively by conspiracy theorists and wild-eyed leftist partisans largely out of touch with reality and looking to slur their opponents with the most outrageous slander possible.

In fact, fascism is a duly recognized school of political thought that leads to governmental authority of a particular type. Although two of its most infamous manifestations of the 20th century were Hitler's Nazi Germany and Franco's Spain, it has been enacted equally as effectively in a number of other countries - Salazar's Portugal, Papadopoulos's Greece, Pinochet's Chile, and Suharto's Indonesia. To be sure, they constitute a mixed bag of national identities, cultures, developmental levels, and histories. But they all followed the fascist or proto-fascist model in obtaining, expanding, and maintaining power.

Researcher Laurence W. Britt has analyzed fascism, in an essay that originally appeared in *Free Inquiry* magazine. It is based on a detailed examination of modern fascist states. Its implications for "freedom and democracy," as they have been known in America, are vitally important. Its relevance to the culture "we the people" are presently living in is terrifying.

Fascism, according to Britt's scholarly research, is defined as follows:

1. Powerful and continuing expressions of nationalism. From the prominent displays of flags and bunting to the ubiquitous lapel pins, the fervor to show patriotic nationalism, both on the part of the regime itself and of citizens caught up in its frenzy, was always obvious. Catchy slogans, pride in the military, and demands for unity were common themes in expressing this nationalism. It was usually coupled with a suspicion of things foreign that often bordered on xenophobia.

2. Disdain for the importance of human rights. The regimes themselves viewed human rights as of little value and a hindrance to realizing the objectives of the ruling elite. Through clever use of propaganda, the population was brought to accept these human rights abuses by marginalizing, even demonizing, those being targeted. When abuse was egregious, the tactic was to use secrecy, denial, and disinformation.

3. Identification of enemies/scapegoats as a unifying cause. The most significant common thread among these regimes was the use of scapegoating as a means to divert the people's attention from other problems, to shift blame for failures, and to channel frustration in controlled directions. The methods of choice – relentless propaganda and disinformation – were usually effective. Often the regimes would incite "spontaneous" acts against the target scapegoats, usually Communists, Socialists, liberals, Jews, ethnic and racial minorities, traditional national enemies, members of other religions, secularists, homosexuals, and "terrorists."

Active opponents of these regimes were inevitably labeled as terrorists and dealt with accordingly.

4. The supremacy of the military/avid militarism. Ruling elites always identified closely with the military and the industrial infrastructure that supported it. A disproportionate share of national resources was allocated to the military, even when domestic needs were acute. The military was seen as an expression of nationalism and was used whenever possible to assert national goals, intimidate other nations, and increase the power and prestige of the ruling elite.

5. Rampant sexism. Beyond the simple fact that the political elite and the national culture were male-dominated, these regimes inevitably viewed women as second-class citizens. They were adamantly anti-abortion and also homophobic. These attitudes were usually codified in Draconian laws that enjoyed strong support by the orthodox religion of the country, thus lending the regime cover for its abuses.

6. A controlled mass media. Under some of the regimes, the mass media were under strict direct control and could be relied upon never to stray from the party line. Other regimes exercised more subtle power to ensure media orthodoxy. Methods included the control of licensing and access to resources, economic pressure, appeals to patriotism, and implied threats. The leaders of the mass media were often politically compatible with the power elite. The result was usually success in keeping the general public unaware of the regimes' excesses.

7. Obsession with national security. Inevitably, a national security apparatus was under direct control of the ruling elite. It was usually an instrument of oppression, operating in secret and beyond any constraints. Its actions were justified under the rubric of protecting "national security," and questioning its activities was portrayed as unpatriotic or even treasonous.

8. Religion and ruling elite tied together. Unlike Communist regimes, the fascist and proto-fascist regimes were never proclaimed as godless by their opponents. In fact, most of the regimes attached themselves to the predominant religion of the country and chose to portray themselves as militant defenders of that religion. The fact that the ruling elite's behavior was incompatible with the precepts of the religion was generally swept under the rug. Propaganda kept up the illusion that the ruling elites were defenders of the faith and opponents of the "godless." A perception was manufactured that opposing the power elite was tantamount to an attack on religion.

9. Power of corporations protected. Although the personal life of ordinary citizens was under strict control, the ability of large corporations to operate in relative freedom was not compromised. The ruling elite saw the corporate structure as a way to not only ensure military production (in developed states), but also as an additional means of social control. Members of the economic elite were often pampered by the political elite to ensure a continued mutuality of interests, especially in the repression of "have-not" citizens.

10. Power of labor suppressed or eliminated. Since organized labor was seen as the one power center that could challenge the political hegemony of the ruling elite and its corporate allies, it was inevitably crushed or made powerless. The poor formed an underclass, viewed with suspicion or outright contempt. Under some regimes, being poor was considered akin to a vice.

11. Disdain and suppression of intellectuals and the arts. Intellectuals and the inherent freedom of ideas and expression associated with them were anathema to these regimes. Intellectual and academic freedom were considered subversive to national security and the patriotic ideal. Universities were tightly controlled, politically unreliable faculty harassed or eliminated. Unorthodox ideas or expressions of dissent were strongly attacked, silenced, or crushed. To these regimes, art and literature should serve the national interest or they had no right to exist.

12. Obsession with crime and punishment. Most of these regimes maintained Draconian systems of criminal justice with huge prison populations. The police were often glorified and had almost unchecked power, leading to rampant abuse. "Normal" and political crime were often merged into trumped-up criminal charges and sometimes used against political opponents of the regime. Fear, and hatred, of criminals or "traitors" was often promoted among the population as an excuse for more police power.

13. Rampant cronyism and corruption. Those in business circles and close to the power elite often used their position to enrich themselves. This corruption worked both ways; the power elite would receive financial gifts and property from the economic elite, who in turn would gain the benefit of government favoritism. Members of the power elite were in a position to obtain vast wealth from other sources as well: for example, by stealing national resources. With the national security apparatus under control and the media muzzled, this corruption was largely unconstrained and not well understood by the general population.

14. Fraudulent elections. Elections in the form of plebiscites or public opinion polls were usually bogus. When actual elections with candidates were held, they would usually be perverted by the power elite to get the desired result. Common methods included maintaining control of the election machinery, intimidating and disenfranchising opposition voters, destroying or disallowing legal votes, and, as a last resort, turning to a judiciary beholden to the power elite.

Does any of this ring alarm bells? Of course not. After all, this is America, officially a democracy with the rule of law, a Constitution, a free press, honest elections, and a well-informed public constantly being put on guard against evil. Historical comparisons like these are just exercises in verbal gymnastics. Maybe, maybe not, Britt concluded.

Chapter 54

Abandoning Humanitarian Traditions

To the average American – particularly those on the right of the political spectrum – such chilling historical analysis of our present-day situation will seem like the latest conspiracy theory. To anyone who undertakes a sincere accounting of his or her country in a time of national crisis, however, such logical deconstruction of Pax Americana will come as a revelation.

What is most important to understand is that the political left in America – the "revolutionary" faction that spawned everything from the post-Depression labor movement to the antiwar movement of the 1960s – has fled in defeat and denial from the truth, and abdicated its social responsibility to provide an effective countermeasure against a Republican insurrection against the Constitution.

"Since mainstream left-liberal media do not seriously ask this question," observed Harvard graduate student Anis Shivani in an October 26, 2002, essay entitled "Is America Becoming Fascist?" for the respected online journal *Counterpunch.org*, "analysis of what has gone wrong and where we are heading has been mostly off-base. Investigation of the kinds of under-handed, criminal tactics fascist regimes undertake to legitimize their agenda and accelerate the rate of change in their favor is dismissed ... Liberals insist that this regime must be treated under the rules of 'politics as usual.' ... If the 'F' word is uttered, liberals are quick to note certain obvious dissimilarities with previous variants of fascism and say that what is happening in America is not fascist.

"... At the liberal *New York Times* or *The Nation*, American writers dare not speak the truth," Shivani declared. He also noted, with striking relevance to today's nascent Holy War, that "Max Frankel, former editor of the *Times*, quotes from biographer Joachim Fest in his review of [a biography of Nazi Albert] *Speer: The Final Verdict*: 'How easily, given appropriate conditions, people will allow themselves to be mobilized into violence, abandoning the humanitarian traditions they have built up over centuries to protect themselves from each other,' and that a 'primal being' such as Hitler 'will always crop up again.' "

The American College Dictionary defines "primal" as "of first importance" or "fundamental." From the deep-seated fear and anxiety still engendered by the horrible memory in the national psyche of the events of 9/11, the militarism of George W. Bush and the PNAC-Dominionists can be seen as salvation, not a crime against humanity of even worse proportion, in turn provoking an even more inhuman response in Iraq – the beheadings of relative innocents.

"How great a deviation from the roots of the enlightenment, the foundations of its self-justification, is the Manichean demonization of enemies, aliens, impure races, and barbaric others?" Shivani asked rhetorically, raising an even more troubling point about the Neocon domination of the peaceful majority of Americans by the violent, militaristic minority. "Nazism never had the support of the majority of Germans; at best about a third fully supported it. About a third of Americans today are certifiably fascist; another 20 percent or so can be swayed around with smart propaganda to particular causes ... Hitler never won clear majorities; yet once he was in power, he crushed all dissent. Consider the parallels to the fateful election of 2000. Hitler's ascent to power was facilitated by the political elites; again, note the similarities to the last two years. Hitler took advantage of the Reichstag fire to totally change the shape of German institutions and culture; think of 9/11 as a close parallel."

George Mosse, a historian and co-author of *International Fascism 1920-45* (Harper Torchbooks, 1966) with Walter Laqueur, "describes fascism as viewing itself in a permanent state of war, to mobilize masculine virile energy, enlisting the masses as 'foot soldiers of a civic religion,' " Shivani noted. "Mosse rejects the notion that fascism ruled through terror: 'It was built upon a popular consensus.' "

Fascist leaders, Mosse explained in his book, as noted by Shivani, "when in opposition, extol traditional values, but they appeal for support to the masses, and exploit any form of mass discontent that is available."

In modern history, perhaps no one – with the obvious exception of Hitler, who had much greater powers of oration and a deeper well of discontent from which to draw – has so masterfully manifested such a simple and self-serving tactic as George W. Bush. Indeed, concluded Shivani six months before the invasion of Iraq, "Bush is the most dangerous man in contemporary history: Hitler didn't have access to weapons that could blow up the world, and no American or other leader since World War II with access to such weapons has been as out of control."

Chapter 55

The Fascist Plot Not Taught in U.S. History

To the average American, who believes that a fascist government could never take hold in the United States, it will come as a jolting revelation to discover that it nearly happened at the same time Hitler came to power, planned and financed by the same elite American families that funded the Nazi dictator's rise.

Buried and quietly forgotten in the Library of Congress and the books of George Seldes, author of *Facts and Fascism* (1945), is the remarkable story of how, in 1933–34, the principals of the most powerful corporations in the U.S. tried to overthrow the U.S. government and depose Franklin Delano Roosevelt in a capitalist coup.

The plan was simple: lure 500,000 unemployed and desperate World War I veterans into a fascist army of domestic revolution, based on the French Croix de Feu ("Cross of Fire"), according to *The Plot to Seize the White House* (Hawthorn Books, 1972), by historian Jules Archer, and other accounts.

Remington Arms, owned by the DuPont family, agreed to provide weapons for the coup. The company had a relationship with Samuel Bush, great-grandfather of President George W. Bush, that dated back to World War I. DuPont Chemical and General Motors, two other giant corporations controlled by the DuPonts, aided and abetted Hitler's rise to power and reaped grotesque profits from their clandestine endeavors, as did the Bushes, Walkers, and Harrimans.

Although the elite conspirators' first choice for an American commander willing to commit treason to help them reach their goal was another legendary soldier, General Douglas MacArthur, a son-in-law of Edward Stotesbury, a key partner of co-conspirator J.P. Morgan, they eventually decided on a recently retired Marine general and two-time Congressional Medal of Honor winner: Smedley Darlington Butler.

"According to retired Representative John W. McCormack, former Speaker of the House," Archer reported in *The Plot to Seize the White House*, "if the late ... General Butler ... had not been a stubborn devotee of democracy, Americans today could conceivably be living under an American Mussolini, Hitler, or Franco ... But school texts that deal with the New Deal are uniquely silent about the powerful Americans who plotted to seize the White House with a private army ... There is strong evidence to suggest that the conspirators may have been too important politically, socially, and economically to be brought to justice after their scheme had been exposed before the McCormack-Dickstein Committee of the House of Representatives. The largely anti-Roosevelt press ... scotched the story as expeditiously as possible by outright suppression, distortion, and attempts to ridicule General Butler's testimony as capricious fantasy."

On July 1, 1933, the retired Butler had been contacted by a shadowy official of the American Legion named Gerald C. MacGuire. Behind the plot that eventually materialized – under the guise of having Butler deliver speeches to veterans on behalf of the American Legion – was the organization's co-founder and sponsor, Grayson Mallet-Provost Murphy, principal of a powerful Wall Street brokerage house and a director of the J.P. Morgan bank, Guaranty Trust. To Murphy and his wealthy peers, Archer wrote, FDR, "if not an actual secret Communist, was dedicated to destroying the nation's capitalist economy by the New Deal ... They were equally appalled by his speech six weeks earlier that the United States would send no more armed forces to Latin America to protect private investments" – a time-honored practice Butler condemned in his "War is a racket" retirement speech.

By the summer of 1934 – after Butler had held off the plotters for a year while deciding what to do about the conspiracy – big business and the press had turned virulently against Roosevelt. At the same time, according to *The Plot to Seize the White House*, the July 1934 issue of Henry Luce's *Fortune* magazine "devoted a whole edition to glorifying Italian fascism ... It was produced by Laird S. Goldsborough, foreign editor for *Time*, who asked *Fortune's* wealthy readers whether fascism [was] achieving in a few years or decades such a conquest of the spirit of man as Christianity achieved only in ten centuries."

"The good journalist," Goldsborough wrote, "must recognize in fascism certain ancient virtues of the race, whether or not they happen to be momentarily fashionable in his own country. Among these are Discipline, Duty, Courage, Glory, Sacrifice." That summer, Archer reported, "it was not difficult to detect the acrid smell of incipient fascism in the corporate air" of the U.S., as "demagogues with apparently inexhaustible funds for propaganda and agitation led 'patriotic' crusades against Communists, Jews, and 'Jewish bankers,' who were alleged to be behind the New Deal."

In other words, the wealthiest and most powerful families in America, and the giant corporations they owned and ran, emulated Hitler, the man they had funded for years and who would become Fuhrer – sovereign ruler of Germany – the following month.

Just as the plot reached its climax, according to Archer, Smedley Butler had a fateful meeting with the key conspirators, including MacGuire; the retired general "exploded that if MacGuire and his backers tried to mount a fascist putsch, he would raise another army of 500,000 veterans to oppose them – and the nation would be plunged into a new civil war."

MacGuire, in response, "revealed that he now had $3 million in working funds and could get $300 million if it were needed," Archer reported. The chief plotter also revealed that he had the backing of Morgan, one of America's wealthiest industrialists. MacGuire also informed a stunned Butler that the press would announce, within several weeks, the plan for a new and better United States government. When Butler asked for more details about the plan, MacGuire told him "it would be described publicly as a society 'to maintain the Constitution.' " From 70 years ago, that rhetoric rings with Orwellian relevance to the Constitution Restoration Act of 2004.

In September 1934, right on schedule, the compliant press announced the creation of the American Liberty League. "They announced their objective was 'to combat radicalism, to teach the necessity of respect for the rights of persons and property, and generally to foster free private enterprise," Archer recounted. "Denouncing the New Deal, they attacked Roosevelt for 'fomenting class hatred,' by using such terms as 'unscrupulous money changers,' 'economic royalists,' and 'the privileged princes of these new economic dynasties.'

"Heavy contributors to the American Liberty League," Archer continued, "included the Pitcairn family (Pittsburgh Plate Glass), Andrew W. Mellon Associates, Rockefeller Associates, E.F. Hutton Associates, William S. Knudsen (General Motors), and the Pew family (Sun Oil Associates), and J. Howard Pew, longtime friend and supporter of Robert Welch, who later founded the John Birch Society."

The earliest supporters of the carefully disguised but clearly fascist American Liberty League included secret Nazi financier Prescott Bush.

Chapter 56

The New York Times Helps Bury the Truth

A fraid that the plot was about to succeed without his military leadership, Smedley Butler revealed the conspiracy to the city editor of *The Philadelphia Record*, a man named Tom O'Neil, who, along with the legendary general, would help save the Constitution from subversion by the rich and powerful. In turn, O'Neil assigned his star reporter, Paul Comly French, to the biggest story of his career.

As French quietly investigated the capitalist coup conspiracy while Butler spoke out against war and profiteering, rumors of the plot reached the McCormack-Dickstein Committee of the U.S. House of Representatives. Headed by future Speaker of the House John W. McCormack, the committee – genesis of the infamous House Un-American Activities Committee that would later lead anti-Communist witch hunts under Senator Joseph McCarthy – was then focused on fascist activities in the U.S.

On November 20, 1934, the committee heard testimony in a secret session in New York City from Butler. At the same time, French reported the scandalous story in *The Philadelphia*

Record and *New York Post*. "Major General Smedley D. Butler revealed today that he has been asked by a group of wealthy New York brokers to lead a fascist movement to set up a dictatorship in the United States," French wrote in his lead. In his testimony before the McCormack-Dickstein Committee – testimony that was later censored – French confirmed that head plotter Gerald C. MacGuire had implicated the DuPont family in a conversation with him. French also testified that the plotters had used the excuse of stopping Communism in the U.S. to justify their treason.

On November 21, 1934, *The New York Times* – under a two-column headline, "General Butler Bares 'Fascist Plot' To Seize Government by Force" – ran a story that perplexed and troubled Butler. He "was struck by a unique arrangement of the facts," Jules Archer wrote in *The Plot to Seize the White House*. "Instead of beginning with a full account of his charges, there was only a brief paragraph restating the facts in the headline. This was followed by a whole string of denials, or ridicule of the charges, by prominent people implicated. Extensive space was given to their attempts to brand Butler a liar or lunatic. Only at the tail of the story, buried inside the paper, did the *Times* wind up its account with a few brief paragraphs mentioning some of his allegations."

The rest of the press, however, dropped the tail when they ran the story. "Newspaper publishers," Archer explained, "had little reason to be fond of the firebrand general who, in his speech to veterans in Atlanta almost a year earlier, had warned them not to believe the capitalist-controlled press."

Lead conspirator MacGuire called the plot "a joke – a publicity stunt. I know nothing about it … I deny the story completely."

Only legendary anti-fascist journalist George Seldes had the courage to report the truth: "All the principals in the case," he wrote in *Facts and Fascism*, "were American Legion officials and financial backers."

As American veterans from across the country demanded prosecution of the plotters, Associated Press did its part to protect them with anti-Smedley Butler propaganda. "On November 22," Archer reported in his book, AP "struck a low blow at Butler by getting Mayor Fiorello LaGuardia of New York to express an opinion of the conspiracy based on what he had read about it in the press." Under the headline " 'Cocktail Putsch,' Mayor Says," AP reported: "Mayor LaGuardia of New York laughingly described today's charges of General Smedley D. Butler that New York brokers suggested he lead an army of 500,000 ex-servicemen on Washington as 'a cocktail putsch.' The Mayor indicated he believed that someone at a party had suggested the idea to the ex-Marine as a joke."

On December 3, 1934, Henry Luce's *Time* ran a cover story entitled "The Plot Without Plotters." Characterized by Archer as a "parody" of the truth and Butler, the *Time* story helped bury the findings of the McCormack-Dickstein Committee. In a 1971 interview for his book, Archer asked McCormack about *Time*'s anti-Butler propaganda. The former Speaker of the House's answer, Archer wrote, "was a snort of disgust. '*Time* has always been about as filthy a publication as ever existed,' he said emphatically. 'I've said that publicly many times. The truth gets no coverage at all, just sensationalism, whatever will sell copies.' "

Meanwhile, back in late 1934, *The New York Times* had also done its part to paint Butler, one of the great heroes in American military history, as a rube who couldn't distinguish reality from fantasy. Only after McCormack-Dickstein Committee co-chairman Samuel Dickstein of New York confronted the *Times* did the paper print a revised final story, one that still failed to disclose the real facts of the conspiracy.

In his 1971 interview with Archer, McCormack said, "The *Times* is the most slanting newspaper in the world. I would not expect anything else from them. They brainwash the American people. It's an empire."

By the time the McCormack-Dickstein Committee issued its final report to a largely silent press, those few reporters, like George Seldes, who cared about truth had turned their attention to another story - rumblings of secret Nazi support and clandestine activities in the U.S. as Hitler came to power. A decade later, Seldes would uncover the Bush-Harriman-Nazi connection, only to discover that no "reputable" U.S. newspaper would publish his stories.

Today, not a word of the Nazi past of the Bush family or the 1934 corporate coup attempt by America's wealthiest families can be found in a high school or college history book or official biography of any of the principals. The public record has been expunged, and alternative-media accounts have been denounced as fraud, perpetrated by traitors.

The 1972 book, *The Plot to Seize the White House*, by a respected historian and biographer of such international figures as Eisenhower, Stalin, and Mao Tse-tung, has effectively vanished from existence.

George Orwell would, no doubt, be awed by that accomplishment.

VII

Disappearing Civics

Chapter 57

Abdicating Our Responsibility as Citizens

In their vast and unequivocal wisdom, America's Founding Fathers spoke and wrote eloquently and relentlessly of democracy's fragility and the role of "we the people" in its defense. "Remember," John Adams wrote in 1814, "democracy never lasts long. It soon wastes, exhausts, and murders itself. There never was a democracy yet that did not commit suicide."

In 1763 – before there was a Revolutionary War or Declaration of Independence or a U.S. Constitution – Adams wrote, in "An Essay on Man's Lust for Power": "Democracy will soon degenerate into an anarchy, such an anarchy that every man will do what is right in his own eyes and no man's life or property or reputation or liberty will be secure, and every one of these will soon mould itself into a system of subordination of all the moral virtues and intellectual abilities, all the powers of wealth, beauty, wit, and science, to the wanton pleasures, the capricious will, and the execrable cruelty of one or a very few."

James Madison, chief framer of the Constitution, wrote in *The Federalist Papers* in 1787: "Democracies have ever been spectacles of turbulence and contention; have ever been found incompatible with personal security, or the rights of property, and have, in general, been as short in their lives as they have been violent in their deaths."

Nevertheless, Madison and Adams and the other few men who bravely and brilliantly set the world on a course toward an unprecedented sort of representative Constitutional republic, pressed on with their admittedly imperfect vision for salvation from the savagery of King George III. Despite the checkered past and limited success of the notion of democracy in history, the creators of the American brand of freedom stamped it with an unmistakable warranty: the will of the people, the consent of the governed, based on an informed and civically involved populace.

"I know of no safe depository of the ultimate powers of the society but the people themselves," Thomas Jefferson wrote in 1820, "and if we think them not enlightened enough to exercise their control with a wholesome discretion, the remedy is not to take it from them, but to inform their discretion by education. This is the true corrective of abuses of constitutional power."

Four years earlier, Jefferson had written in another letter, "Enlighten the people generally, and tyranny and oppression of body and mind will vanish like spirits at the dawn of day."

In 2004, with such a body of thought as basis, one must wonder what Jefferson and his Constitutional cohorts would think of events of the day and the public's reaction – or lack thereof. As long-cherished Constitutional freedoms are evaporated under the Orwellian Patriot Act, as a sitting President of the United States refuses to atone for the fact he led the nation to war based on lies and subterfuge, as American workers lose their jobs to the sinister practice called outsourcing, "we the people" sit idly by – uninformed, distracted, and shamefully compliant in a conspiracy of silence that will almost surely confirm, eventually if not soon, the musings of Madison, Adams, and Jefferson.

Of the many reasons "we the people" have today for profound distress over our future, none is greater than the fact that we have abdicated our responsibilities as citizens. We have failed to live up to the high and demanding standard put forth in the speeches and documents that form our precious national heritage. Perhaps the most distressing example of our failure is our defeatist cynicism, our belief, consciously or unconsciously, that the Fortune 500, not "we the people," own the government, and that truth and honor no longer matter to our national character.

Of all the fears and anxieties that imposed themselves upon Madison, Adams, and Jefferson, and the rest of our forefathers, it is likely that none would so horrify them as such hard, undeniable truth. More than anything else, they feared that the many would end up being ruled by the few, and that special interests – called "factions" back then – would dominate the populace on the fields of political battle.

"The most sacred of the duties of a government [is] to do equal and impartial justice to all citizens," Jefferson wrote in an 1816 note. If that is true, and surely it is, Jefferson must be looking down upon us from the cosmos and bemoaning the "postmodern" insensitivity and exclusion shown to African-Americans, Native Americans, the homeless, the mentally ill, the working poor, and the growing general population of the disenfranchised.

As for their shared abhorrence of preferential treatment for any class of citizens, John Adams wrote in *Thoughts on Government* in 1776: "Government is instituted for the common good; for the protection, safety, prosperity, and happiness of the people; and not for profit, honor, or private interest of any one man, family, or class of men. Therefore, the people alone have an incontestable, unalienable, and indefeasible right to institute government; and to reform, alter, or totally change the same, when their protection, safety, prosperity, and happiness require it."

Today, we find ourselves in a civic dilemma: The Congress, poisoned by greed and special interests, bloated on a diet of pork, no longer represents "the common citizen." Instead, most of our Representatives and Senators, of both parties, cater to corporate interests, at the daily expense of "we the people," by pawning our once-revered heritage to million-dollar lobbyists and special-interest groups. The token payment reflected on our national pawn ticket amounts to nothing more than enough for mere survival, while those who control the transnational corporations receive incomes and amass personal fortunes almost beyond the comprehension of the "common" man or woman.

And what do "we the people" do?

Nothing.

We sit by, bemoan our abuse at the hands of those empowered to protect and serve our best interests, and tune in – for nothing other than pathetic escapism – to *Survivor* or *The Bachelor* or *The Apprentice*, "reality TV" that makes a mockery of reality. At work, we don't discuss the troubling implications of Patriot Act II or the now-disastrous "Bush Doctrine" that has led us to Holy War in Iraq; instead we speculate on whether Kobe Bryant raped his concierge in a luxury lodge, or whether Satanists beheaded Laci Peterson.

As a result, we get the dysfunctional government we deserve.

In truth, if Jefferson and company were right, it is unfair of us to blame the Bush administration, or bureaucrats, or liberals, or Neocon Republicans.

We must blame ourselves.

We must accept responsibility.

Most of all, however, we must act.

But first, as Jefferson noted, we must be enlightened.

Chapter 58

A Real-Life Lesson from a Fictional Town

I n the pre-George W. Bush world of the late 1990s, a Waco, Texas, high-school student named Courtney Beuerlein crafted what is perhaps the perfect metaphor for the state of the Union in the early 21st century.

"Welcome to Dowersville, Texas," Beuerlein wrote in a national essay contest on why young Americans, their sense of patriotism suffocated by cynicism, are losing their enthusiasm for the vote. "Yesterday was Election Day in Dowersville, and our federal representative to Congress was elected by one vote. Today, Adam Dowager, the new representative, called a press conference to discuss his plans and goals as our representative. Mr. Dowager announced that he would push to cut off financial aid to college students by 75 percent, which would cut down on the number of students in college, allowing those that could afford it the best possible education.

"Now, Dowersville is home to Dowersville State College, which would lose almost half of its enrollment under Mr. Dowager's plan. How did this happen? Well, Dowersville has almost 100,000 people between the ages of 18 and 25, yet only 10,000 were registered to vote, and of those registered only 337 voted."

Although national statistics on voter turnout are not as dire as in Beuerlein's angry satirical essay, they are nevertheless grim for anyone who clings to any notion of "we the people." In 1998, according to the New Millennium Survey undertaken by the National Information Consortium, fewer than one in five Americans between the ages of 18 and 24 chose to vote. In 2000, just 46 percent of that age group voted in the critical Presidential election, which only generated an overall turnout of 51 percent, according to the Federal Election Commission (FEC). Since 1972, participation by young voters has declined by about 13 percent – the largest drop of any age group.

The reason is clear, and it now affects disgruntled adults as much as young people. Put bluntly, a growing number of Americans no longer believe in the precious system of representative democracy for which our ancestors fought and died.

There were 205,815,000 citizens of voting age in 2000; of the 156,421,311 registered to vote, only 105,586,274 actually voted. That means that 100,228,726 U.S. citizens of voting age, whether registered or not, failed to partake of their opportunity to have a direct voice in their government.

Why?

In the New Millennium Survey, the two primary reasons why young people said they did not vote were that they didn't think their vote makes any difference, and that they didn't have enough "information" to vote. Considering that our 70 million-plus 18- to 24-year-olds populate a generation larger than the Baby Boom generation, such a reality is devastating to any idea of government "of the people, by the people, and for the people." In today's world of post-George W. Bush alienation and despair, young people categorically reject any such idea of who owns their government.

"Youth are disillusioned with politics for many of the same reasons that our parents are," Taiwan-born University of California at Berkeley student Jim C. Fung wrote in his essay, which won the college division of the same essay contest in which Beuerlein created her imaginary Texas town. "If lobbyists and campaign contributors did not have more access to public officials than do regular citizens; if economic democracy in the workplace existed alongside what some would call the 'illusion' of political democracy; if elected officials acted more on 'bread and butter' economic issues, such as the increasing concentration of wealth and the lack of health insurance for many Americans, than on expanding the prison population and on the military, most people of all ages would consider their votes much more meaningful."

In yet another essay, high-school winner Matthew Carlson of Snohomish, Washington, wrote: "In many Presidential elections, numerous Americans have found themselves compromising their views and voting for the candidate who they dislike the least. This compromise that is forced upon the electorate is a result of the two-party system on which we rely for voting simplicity … An anonymous Vermont farmer, when asked by a [National Public Radio] reporter which Presidential candidate he would be likely to vote for in the 2000 election, responded by stating that he honestly did not care who the President was because they were essentially all the same, and none of them would represent him fairly."

Later in his essay, Fung noted, "Democracy can only exist when the citizens of a democratic state are willing and able to take an active role in their government." Many of his fellow essayists made the same point, yet no one has offered a genuine solution to the problem.

In fact, it is not the "system" that is broken. It is "we the people" that are broken. It is our social and political will, as owners and self-rulers of our country, that must be restored.

There is nothing wrong with our electoral system, except that half of us fail to vote, and many of us who do vote do so without the information we need to cast our ballot effectively. In their genius, our Founding Fathers left a legacy of freedom and democracy that is flawless in its conception. The problem "we the people" face today is a partisanship that has poisoned the well of "common good."

The fact is that like it or not, "we the people," enslaved by material consumption, distracted by debt and stress, have abdicated our most sacred and profound responsibility as citizens: electing men and women to public office who are worthy and capable of truly representing our shared best interests against the caprices of the "postmodern" capitalist world of the 21st century – and accepting nothing less.

Chapter 59
Falling Short of Equality and Justice

"In every human society, there is an effort continually tending to confer on one part the height of power and happiness, and to reduce the other to the extreme of weakness and misery," Adolph Caso wrote in the introduction to his 1995 book, *We the People: Formative Documents of America's Democracy*. "The intent of good laws is to oppose this effort, and to diffuse their influence universally and equally. But men generally abandon the care of their most important concerns to the uncertain prudence and discretion of those whose interest it is to reject the best and wisest institutions, and it is not until they have been led into a thousand mistakes in matters, the most essential to their lives and liberties, and are weary of suffering, that they can be induced to apply a remedy to the evils with which they are oppressed.

"It is then," Caso concluded, "they begin to conceive and acknowledge the most palpable truths, which ... commonly escape vulgar minds incapable of analyzing objects ... accustomed to receiving impressions without distinction ...

to be determined rather by the opinions of others, than by the result of their own examination."

Those words amount to a scathing indictment of the American citizenry of 2004.

"Although the words 'we the people' suggest that the Constitution applies equally to all Americans," Caso continued, "the attainment of that equality has fallen short for most people … Certainly [such equality] was not achieved with the ratification of the Constitution, neither with the issuance of the Emancipation Proclamation, nor with the ratification of the 19th Amendment, nor with so much civil rights legislation. Yet, the Founding Fathers, knowing their own limitations, have projected their idealism through various documents, leaving to their [descendants] to *fulfill the nation's idealism through proper deeds of their own"* [emphasis added].

Not long after there was a U.S. Constitution – and newly created free citizens were already fighting among themselves over the issues of the day – John Adams recorded his thoughts on those who would blame "the government" rather than take responsibility themselves. "The declaration that our people are hostile to a government made by ourselves and for themselves, and conducted by themselves, is an insult," Adams wrote.

A great Italian thinker of the 18th century, Giacinto Dragonetti – quoted by Thomas Paine in his pivotal 1776 treatise *Common Sense* – had already established a general ethic for effective public government. "The science of the politician," Dragonetti wrote, "consists in fixing the true point of happiness and freedom. Those men would deserve the gratitude of ages, who should discover a mode of government that contained the greatest sum of individual happiness, with the least national expense."

By that standard, how effective would you say the present government of the United States is?

Dragonetti also noted the same caution that caused James Madison to observe that "knowledge will forever govern ignorance": "Be sure that wise men be the companions of liberty," Dragonetti warned. "The evils that arise from knowledge are in inverse ratio to their diffusion, whereas the benefits are in direct ratio."

By that standard, the United States of America is in *big* trouble, facing complex and nagging problems that require creative, ethical solutions – just as did the tyranny of King George III and the British East India Company. But before "we the people" can create solutions in which we all share an equal stake, we must first admit the true nature of the problem.

It is not because George W. Bush has been President, or because Social Security and Medicare are going broke, or because so many jobs are being exported to low-wage countries such as India. It is because "we the people" have allowed those things to happen in our names, and in memory of Jefferson, Madison, and Paine, among others.

It is because we have allowed our common national interests – family, home, community, decency – to splinter into "partisan" political "issues" and polarized "debate," while giant transnational corporate interests have single-mindedly and relentlessly used million-dollar lobbyists to subvert the entire U.S. government and the political process itself, right in front of our eyes.

It is because instead of fighting for the common good, we have fought only for the "personal" issues that drive us – for or against abortion, for or against gun control, for or against gay marriage – while the Fortune 500 has pursued but one goal: economic domination of the planet and all the human beings who inhabit it.

We have sat by and watched as our highest government officials have lied to and betrayed us in order to satisfy their greed, while we look the other way and satisfy our own greed with bigger homes and more tricked-out SUVs, while millions of Americans struggle to remain above the poverty line and the disenfranchised struggle simply to survive in the wealthiest nation in the history of the world.

As a consequence, "we the people" have gotten the government we deserve - and it is a miserably dysfunctional one at this point.

The essential question now, as posed by the great Russian writer Leo Tolstoy a century ago, is: "What is to be done?"

Instead of working toward real answers to that question, we have deluded ourselves into believing in the myths of "American affluence" and "economic growth." The delusion has been created largely by a compliant corporate media that instead of disseminating real "news" - information we need in order to do a more effective job of living our lives and leaving the world a better place for our children – have given us brain-numbing propaganda, perpetuated by the handful of billionaires who now own virtually all of our TV and cable networks, newspapers, and magazines. As such, they control public opinion – and, feeling defeated and helpless, we do nothing to regain control of our "reality."

Mark Twain – once again a source of simple and timeless inspiration – noted that "a lie can travel halfway around the world while the truth is still puttin' on its shoes."

It's time for the American people to put shoes on the truth.

Then it's time, as a nation, to find genuine solutions – rather than empty slogans in 30-second political ads – for problems that are largely ignored by the career professional politicians who must sell their souls to corporate special interests and millionaire lobbyists in order to get elected in the first place.

VIII

Solving the Problem

Chapter 60

If You're Not Outraged, You're Not Paying Attention

"A s Abraham Lincoln biographer Albert J. Beveridge noted in 1928," Thom Hartmann wrote in *Unequal Protection: The Rise of Corporate Dominance and the Theft of Human Rights,* 'Facts when justly arranged interpret themselves.' "

If "we the people" are ever to face the justly arranged facts about our past, our present, and – most important – our future, we must address the reality of "postmodern" America in a way that allows for a clear, non-partisan, non-political interpretation. It is only by such initiative that we can ever recapture the spirit of the United States, as intended by our Founding Fathers and subverted by corporations and the corrupt government that has enthroned them as our true rulers.

"A popular bumper sticker," Wilbur M. Rhodes of Kittery, Maine, wrote in the newsletter of the Boston & Cambridge Alliance for Democracy (BCAD) earlier this year, "reads, 'If you are not outraged, you are not paying attention.' If you are not paying attention and doing nothing to reverse [current events], you will continue to be the victim of a Congress and an Administration that is run by the short-sighted greed of those who will destroy our country and the world." The letter, titled "Impeach Congress, Too" and signed by 34 other members of the BCAD, appeared in the June 18 edition of *The New Hampshire Gazette*.

More than 70 years before that – just before Adolf Hitler rose to power – Aldous Huxley, another visionary allegorist, alongside George Orwell in his opposition to state tyranny, wrote in *Brave New World*: "The greatest triumphs of propaganda have been accomplished, not by doing something, but by refraining from doing. Great is truth, but still greater, from a practical point of view, is silence about truth."

Three decades later, Martin Luther King, Jr. would observe, during America's greatest spiritual crisis since the Civil War, the civil rights movement, that "history will have to record that the greatest tragedy of this period of social transition was not the strident clamor of the bad people, but the appalling silence of the good people."

In 1932, two years before the wealthiest families in the U.S. would try to overthrow the government and impose a Hitler-style fascist regime, Albert Einstein wrote in a letter to Sigmund Freud: "The minority, the ruling class at present, has the schools and the press, usually the church as well, under its thumb. This enables it to organize and sway the emotions of the masses and make its tool of them."

In 1776, in perhaps his most famous proclamation, Thomas Paine wrote in *The Crisis*: "These are the times that try men's souls. The summer soldier and the sunshine patriot will, in this crisis, shrink from the services of their country, but he that stands it *now* deserves the love and thanks of man and woman."

Today, America is in crisis. Unlike 1776, however, the average American neither seems to recognize that fact, nor have any truly patriotic reaction to it. Instead, Republicans blame Democrats, liberals blame conservatives, Christians demonize Muslims, and militant Muslims wreak havoc on the world to defend themselves from inhuman aggression that "we the people" approve of in opinion polls as a "War on Terror," in response to the national tragedy of 9/11.

What we must realize – and fight against, in a new and robust American Revolution, based not on weaponry but on truth, not on warfare but on compassion and understanding – is that the *real* war is being waged, by both parties, and by both extremes of the political spectrum, against the Constitution and the legitimate interests of "we the people" and the developing world.

What, then, to invoke again Tolstoy's timeless question, is to be done?

Given the apparent complexity of our times, the answer is remarkably simple. We must take *action*, across political, demographic, and religious divides, to reach common cause with common sense. We have been sold the myth that our problems are enormously complex, and by definition of that complexity, almost unsolvable. Nothing could be further from the truth.

Here, then, in its simplest possible form, is a non-partisan agenda for positive change and a sustainable society for future generations of Americans.

We must end the corporate stranglehold on government and politics. This is the single most important step required to create a true "government of the people, by the people, and for the people," as envisioned by our Founding Fathers. Today, we have government of the corporation, by the corporation, and for the corporation. That reality is the single greatest crisis we face as a nation.

In his book *When Corporations Rule the World*, economic reform activist David C. Korten outlined a set of simple principles that must be codified into new law:

- Sovereignty resides only in people.
- Corporations have no natural or inalienable rights.
- The problem is the system. The whole system of institutional power must be transformed.

- The Ecological Revolution is a revolution of ideas, not guns.

In offering a genuine vision for a better world, Korten also made a number of companion points. We must, he wrote, undertake several specific initiatives:

End corporate welfare. "Corporate subsidies range from resource depletion allowances to subsidized grazing fees, export subsidies, and tax abatements," he noted. "Such subsidies should be systematically identified and eliminated, with the exception of those needed to establish and nurture locally owned, community-based enterprises" as a countermeasure against giant corporations like Wal-Mart and Starbucks.

Tax shifting. "One of the most basic, but often violated, principles of tax policy is that taxes should be assessed against activities that contribute to social and environmental dysfunction," Korten explained. "Therefore, taxes should be revised to *reduce* taxes on activities that benefit society, such as employment (including employer contributions to Social Security, health care, and worker's compensation). The lost revenue would be made up by taxing activities that contribute to social and environmental dysfunction, such as resource extraction, packaging, pollution, and imports," among others. He also suggested new taxes on things such as pollution emissions and the extraction of virgin materials.

Rigorous enforcement of anti-trust laws. "Vigorous legal action should be taken to break up concentrations of corporate power," Korten wrote. "There should be a legal presumption that any acquisition or merger reduces competition and is contrary to market principles and public interest. The burden of proving otherwise to skeptical regulators should fall squarely on those presenting such proposals." Today, unfortunately, the opposite is true under the errant watch of the Federal Trade Commission.

In *Unequal Protection*, Thom Hartmann suggested that we must:

End corporate personhood, by reversing the little-known and grossly misinterpreted 1886 Supreme Court decision, *Santa Clara County v. Southern Pacific Railroad.* Corporations must be held accountable to the people of the communities in which they reside.

Undertake a new entrepreneurial boom, a wave of sustainable small businesses that grow to serve legitimate human needs and interests and create good, secure jobs.

In addition, says international businessman and former mayor of Berlin, New Hampshire, Richard Bosa, we must replace the multinational corporate business model with a local cooperative model under which manufacturing plants and other industrial facilities that do not make muster for a corporate bottom line can be reborn under community or employee ownership. "Employees vote for members of the company's board of directors," Bosa explained. "All major projects and funding decisions must be approved by the majority of the owner-stockholder employees, who 'own' their jobs directly. It's a model that produces a team spirit, better productivity, less supervision, and more innovation. The company is part of the community, so issues such as pollution and protection of the environment are considered more important." As a good example, Bosa cited Marland Mold, Inc. of Pittsfield, Massachusetts: "The workers bought the company and have remained successful even when the economy has taken a downturn."

We must also withdraw from international trade agreements such as NAFTA, the WTO, and FTAA, in favor of *genuine* free trade practices that benefit human beings and communities over giant corporations and world economic superpowers, dominated by the U.S. Fortune 500.

Chapter 61

A Simple Agenda:
Common Sense in a Common Cause

We **must outlaw political action committees and professional lobbying**. "If a lawyer was arguing a case before a judge and said, 'Your honor, before you decide on the guilt or innocence of my client, here is $1,000,' what would we call that?" Janice Fine wrote in *Dollars and Sense* magazine. "We would call that a bribe. But if an industry lobbyist walks into the office of a key legislator and hands him or her a check for $1,000, we call that that a campaign contribution. We should call it a bribe." The only way to cure the cancer of lobbyists and other corporate-controlled political entities is to make them illegal. Only people should have a voice, just as only people have a vote. Professional lobbying and corporate meddling in the electoral process must be stopped – period. Otherwise, "we the people" have no chance of reclaiming our government.

We must hold corporations accountable for their actions. The public trust is compromised when corporate interests supercede the interests of the people. As a result, we must introduce new measures to hold corporations accountable to their public charter. Corporations that violate the interests of the public must be prosecuted, in the name of the American people, by the U.S. Department of Commerce – and face revocation of their corporate charters.

"From the founding of America to the late 1800s, governments routinely revoked corporate charters, forcing liquidation and sale of assets," Thom Hartmann noted in *Unequal Protection.* As an example, Hartmann wrote, "Banks were shut down for behaving in a 'financially unsound' way in Ohio, Mississippi, and Pennsylvania." As late as 1942, the U.S. government took action against errant corporations, such as the Nazi-front enterprises managed by Prescott Bush and the Harrimans and seized, then liquidated, them.

We must end war profiteering by former government officials and Washington insiders. We must require that all U.S. defense contractors adhere to a strict new policy of financial "transparency," monitored on behalf of the American people by new Congressional subcommittees in both the House and Senate, which release annual public reports audited by the General Accounting Office. We must make it illegal for former government officials to participate in defense-related, for-profit businesses that produce unnecessary weapons sold in a climate of fear and militaristic propaganda. We must create a Citizens Defense Oversight Board to consist of defense and aerospace executives, trade journalists, academicians, scientists, and private citizens to represent the full spectrum of society's interests in defense policy.

We must enact a sane defense policy. We must reassess defense policy in the post-Cold War period, when our true enemy is international terrorism, not traditional nationalist military forces. We must reduce the defense budget by at least 25 percent and reinvest that money – $100 billion a year at present – in domestic spending for the common good.

In addition, according to James Carville in his 2003 book *Had Enough? A Handbook for Fighting Back* (Simon & Schuster), in order to reverse the damage done to defense policy and our world image under George W. Bush, we must restore:

The Comprehensive Test Ban Treaty (CTBT) – signed by Bill Clinton in 1996 and opposed by Bush "from day one," Carville explained. "The CTBT would ban all nuclear explosions. Back in 1961, Dwight Eisenhower said that not achieving a nuclear test ban 'would have to be classed as the greatest disappointment of any administration, of any decade, of any time, and of any party.' Bush dismissed it as 'unenforceable.' "

*Anti-Ballistic Missile Trea*ty – in force since 1972, abandoned by George Bush, Carville noted. "The treaty limited the U.S. and Soviets to deploying a single, land-based system to defend against long-range ballistic missiles." Bush abandoned it because he and the PNAC war profiteers now want to arm space, called by Earth Day founder John McConnell "the single most dangerous idea of our time" and opposed by many scientists and former NASA astronauts.

Nuclear Non-Proliferation Treaty (NPT) – in force since 1970, undermined by Bush since 2001. The militaristic administration has since spoken publicly of the possible need to use nuclear weapons, even in a first strike – a concept unheard of until he took office. Bush has also repealed the ban on low-yield nuclear weapons.

Protocol to the Biological Weapons Convention (BWC) – negotiated by the United States for 10 years, abandoned by Bush in July 2001. The BWC, Carville wrote, is "a treaty banning the production, possession, and use of germ warfare agents ... For the last ten years, the U.S. had participated in an effort ... that would get tough on cheaters. In July 2001, the Bush administration announced that it opposed the draft rules that had resulted from those negotiations." In light of our invasion of Iraq – and that Saddam Hussein first acquired his chemical and biological weapons capabilities from the U.S. when George H.W. Bush was Vice President under Ronald Reagan – this is perhaps the single greatest act of hypocrisy by George Bush II.

International Criminal Court (ICC) – "supported by every American administration since World War II, the Bush administration withdrew our signature from the treaty on May 6, 2002," Carville noted. Given the ongoing civilian casualties in Iraq and Afghanistan and the Abu Ghraib and Guantanamo Bay prisoner torture scandals, one can only assume Bush's intent was to protect U.S. officials at the Pentagon and State Department, as well as himself, from any possibility of prosecution for war crimes and other violations of international law.

Conference on the Illicit Trade in Small Arms and Light Weapons in All Its Aspects – conceived July 2001, rejected by Bush outright, Carville wrote. "This was the first attempt by the international community to address the illegal trade in small arms and light weapons – the weapons that fuel civil wars, terrorism, and the international drug trade. These are the kinds of weapons used to kill our troops in Somalia, Afghanistan, and Iraq." The Bush family began its century-long history of war profiteering under Samuel Bush, great-grandfather of George W. Bush, in partnership with Remington Arms, the treasonous corporation that offered to provide weapons for the 1934 fascist overthrow of the U.S. government.

Chapter 62

Correcting Some of Our Worst Policy Mistakes

We must enact a sane foreign policy. Under George W. Bush and the PNAC-Dominionists, the U.S. claims – in Orwellian double-speak – to be exporting "freedom and democracy." In fact, our three primary allies in the Middle East (Egypt, Israel, and Saudi Arabia) are among the most repressive governments on earth and among its worst human-rights violators. Despite Bush administration claims that "Islamic extremists" are responsible for international terrorism, the real cause is U.S. hypocrisy and repression of Muslims, which has empowered Osama bin Laden, as CIA analyst "Anonymous" noted last June in media interviews for his book, *Imperial Hubris: Why the West Is Losing the War on Terror*. In Saudi Arabia, public beheadings and dismemberment for crimes are official policy, yet the Bush administration and the corporate media remain silent about that reality, while condemning al Qaeda as "barbarians" for the beheadings of a few Americans.

To restore America's reputation and rightful place as a moral force in the world, we must put our "allies" on notice that we will not tolerate any further human rights abuses or police-state power.

In his book *Sharing the Land of Canaan: Human Rights and the Israeli-Palestinian Struggle* (Pluto Press) earlier this year, Mazin B. Qumsiyeh invoked George Washington from his farewell address to the nation he had helped found. The passage resonates with relevance in an age when American foreign policy, dating back decades, has become its own worst enemy, not just in the Middle East, but around the world.

"A passionate attachment of one nation for another produces a variety of evils," Washington said. "Sympathy for the favorite nation, facilitating the illusion of an imaginary common interest in cases where no real common interest exists, and infusing into one the enmities of the other, betrays the former into a participation in the quarrels and wars of the latter without adequate inducement or justification. It leads also to concessions to the favorite nation of privileges denied to others which is apt doubly to injure the nation making the concessions; by unnecessarily parting with what ought to have been retained, and by exciting jealousy, ill-will, and a disposition to retaliate, in the parties from whom equal privileges are withheld."

Therein lies a cogent analysis, from more than 200 years ago, of our hypocritical and increasingly harmful entanglements with Israel, Egypt, and Saudi Arabia, among others. In Israel, we support a near-police state, run by a known war criminal (Ariel Sharon) responsible for the deaths of countless innocent Palestinians – women and children – over the past 50 years. In Egypt, we breed hatred in its Muslim ghettoes while proclaiming it an ally to American values. In Saudi Arabia, because we are hopelessly and helplessly addicted to its oil, we ignore the fact that the House of Saud is arguably the most repressive – and violent – regime on the face of the earth.

In the meantime, ill-informed Americans, in the name of the sort of "patriotism" the legendary Emma Goldman wrote about a century ago, send angry e-mails to CNN and Fox

News, in the aftermath of a few beheadings of Americans, demanding that we "exterminate" the "animals" and "savages" of al Qaeda.

If America has any hope of recovery and redemption from its sins against the world, first we must realize that it was not Osama bin Laden who began the Holy War. It was the United States of America, under former President George Herbert Walker Bush, who sent foreign troops to Muslim Holy Lands for the first time since the 7th century.

On September 11, 2001, bin Laden took his revenge. Since then, many thousands of innocent Muslims – non-combatants, human beings who worship the same God as Christians and Jews – have perished at the hands of our high-tech warfare.

For generations to come – unless the Christian Dominionists get their way and end the world *now* – we will pay a terrible price for our ongoing savagery.

We must end illegal immigration. Under George W. Bush, our national borders, most notably with Mexico, have been opened to an unprecedented invasion. Among other ills, increasing illegal immigration – a Bush administration gift to corporations who want cheap labor without benefits – has devastated state and local economies by leading to lower wages for the most impoverished Americans and unleashing a torrent of expensive health care and social services costs paid for by U.S. taxpayers. The ease with which the Mexican border can be transgressed is also an open invitation to terrorists.

Chapter 63
Facing Our Toughest Challenges

We **must reform the media**. We must hold "news" organizations ethically and legally accountable for the fairness and accuracy of their reporting. We must reinstate and update the FCC Fairness Doctrine, mandating that "fair and balanced reporting" be a daily reality on the public airwaves, *not* a trademarked ad slogan for a right-wing propaganda machine like Fox News.

We must break up, under anti-trust law, the media conglomerates that are owned by giant transnational corporations, thereby creating an inherent conflict of interests, and foster a return to local ownership of media. We must roll back the new FCC rules easing conglomerate ownership of the entire U.S. media, including in local markets. We must make the FCC broadcast license renewal process more directly accountable to the local communities the broadcasters serve. Just as revocation of their public charters should be the ultimate punishment for errant corporations, revocation of their broadcast licenses – in the name of "we the people" – ought to be the punishment for

TV stations that undermine public dialogue with consistently biased or inaccurate news reporting.

"What we need to do," Robert McChesney wrote in *Into the Buzzsaw*, "is change the cues so it is rational to produce great journalism. That means we must redouble our efforts to support *independent* media ... Ultimately we need to press for the overhaul of the media system, so that it serves democratic values rather than the interests of capital ... The media system is the result of laws, government subsidies, and regulations made in the public's name, but made corruptly behind closed doors without the public's informed consent ... Our job is to make media reform part of our broader struggle for democracy and social justice. It is impossible to conceive of a better world with a media system that remains under the thumb of Wall Street and Madison Avenue, under the thumb of the ruling class."

Washington Post media writer Howard Kurtz, in his book, *Media Circus*, suggested that journalists "make people mad - write about outrages and injustice ... Tell us things the authorities don't want us to know – we've become so obsessed with the latest middle-class comforts that we've drifted from our original mission of afflicting the comfortable." Kurtz also recommended that the press "liberate the op-ed pages – throw open the gates to new, vibrant, even radical voices ... Connect with the community – we need to give people a sense that we're listening."

Most important, perhaps, there should be an entrepreneurial movement toward fiercely independent local newspapers and other media outlets that embody the editorial spirit of *The New Hampshire Gazette*.

We must restore government to the American people and take it away from special interests. We must create new incentives for citizens who run for office or participate in a political campaign. We must encourage more – and better – candidates for office, at all levels of government, from among "common citizens," including women, minorities, young people, and the disenfranchised.

We must restore the Bill of Rights and all Constitutional protections lost under George W. Bush. Under the Bush administration, basic American freedoms, consecrated by the blood of U.S. veterans to defend our unique Constitutional protections, have been eroded. In the wake of 9/11, Bush, Cheney, and Ashcroft have virtually redefined the concepts of due process and fair and open proceedings, both against "enemy combatants" and U.S. citizens. We must rescind the Patriot Act and roll back all of the provisions put in place that threaten our civil liberties. We must demand a thorough and vigorous independent investigation of the unanswered questions about 9/11 and what lessons we must learn from those tragic events and their ongoing aftermath.

We must shift the tax burden from the middle class to giant corporations and wealthy individuals who presently pay little or no taxes. We must aggressively enforce the U.S. tax code, close all loopholes, and prevent U.S. corporations and wealthy individuals from reducing or avoiding federal taxes by going offshore. We must create a new "wealth tax" so that the super-rich pay their slightly disproportionate "fair share" toward the common good of society, as originally intended when the income tax was first conceived in the early 20th century.

We must ease and simplify the tax burden of the middle class, and increase the "floor" for paying any federal income tax at all to $20,000 per year, thereby lifting millions of minimum-wage working families above the poverty line and giving them a fair chance in life.

We must protect and enforce the separation of church and state. Given the insidious influence of the religious right, we must codify the separation with a Constitutional amendment that will protect our Constitutional freedoms from religious fanatics. At the same time, we must reinforce the traditional religious protections that are at the core of American democracy. Finally, we must expose the Constitution Restoration Act of 2004 and defeat it, while exposing those members of Congress who sponsored it in the first place and the corporate media that failed to report on it so that the public could be aware of its threat to the very thing it professes to protect.

We must hold Congress accountable for its partnership in crime with the executive branch. We must make public heroes of Representatives like Henry Waxman (D-CA), Bernie Sanders (I-VT), and Jim McDermott (D-WA), and Senators Byron Dorgan (D-SD) and Robert Byrd (D-WVA), as well as the few Republicans, including Dana Rohrabacher (R-CA), who truly embody the spirit of our Founding Fathers – and *kick the rest out*. Such high standards, as set by those few, must be met by all – or they must be impeached and removed from office.

In the cynical political environment of 2004, we must remember the words of John Adams from an 1809 letter: "To believe all men honest would be folly. To believe none so, is something worse."

We must clean up and improve the electoral process. We must address the reality that a "fair and open" election process designed to bring honest, capable candidates to office has been corrupted by a "two-party" system – and lobbyists – dependent only on money as its motivating force. Elections must be publicly financed, with spending limits imposed, and electronic voting machines banned in favor of paper ballots. Phoenix talk-radio host Meria Heller has proposed an excellent idea to restore confidence in the American people after the electoral disaster of 2000: count ballots on live local television.

"In return for their right to use public airways," David C. Korten proposed in *When Corporations Rule the World*, "television and radio stations should be required to provide exposure for candidates for public office on issues-oriented interview programs and debates, on an equal-time basis." Such an innovative initiative would enormously enhance the erudition of the electorate.

We must also make one simple, practical change to the electoral system – instant run-off voting, which will make every ballot count in the final results of all elections.

As for electronic voting machines, Boss Tweed, one of the most corrupt political figures in American history, once observed: "As long as I count the votes, what are you going to do about it?"

We must become informed on the issues and VOTE. This is the single most important initiative for the return of government to "we the people" in a way that will effect positive change. We must create new voter registration drives to increase dramatically participation in all elections, from local to federal, as a basic civic duty. The most important reform? We must follow the examples of Australia and Belgium and impose a reasonable penalty for *not* voting – inability to renew one's driver's license.

Chapter 64

New Hope: The Long-Overdue Redistribution of Wealth

I f there is a single idea that is vital to the future of America – aside from increasing voter awareness and turnout in order to inject new life into representative democracy – it is a workable, fair model for the redistribution of wealth.

While no reasonable person would deny that a certain minority of people – either by birthright, hard work, innovation, talent, or providence – have an unalienable right to be rich among a nation of lesser mortals, by the same token, no reasonable person would argue that the widening gap between the haves and have-nots is anything but a formula for social disintegration.

In recent years, three separate but equally interesting models have been put forth.

The first is presented by James Carville in his book, *Had Enough?* It is known as the American Stakeholder Account. "By the end of the 1990s," Carville noted, "the bottom 40 percent of Americans earned just 10 percent of the nation's income and owned less than 1 percent of the nation's wealth.

As progressives, we know that if we don't bring those people into the fold, we'll create an America that is even more separate and unequal. As pragmatists, we know that without the contributions of 40 percent of our country, we'll never get the kind of sustained growth we need." Crediting the concept to Ray Boshara, director of the asset-building program at the New America Foundation – which "brings a lot of smart people and new ideas to Washington," Carville noted – "Every one of the four million babies born in America each year would receive an endowment of $6,000 in an American Stakeholder Account. If invested in a relatively safe portfolio that yielded a 7 percent annual return, this sum would grow to more than $20,000 by the time the child graduated from high school, and to $45,000 by the time he or she reached 30." Funds would be limited to such activities as higher education or vocational training, buying a first home, starting a small business, and ... eventually creating a nest egg for retirement."

In his book, *When Corporations Rule the World*, David C. Korten touted a related but different idea – guaranteed income. "An idea long popular with both conservative and progressive economists," he wrote, "a guaranteed income merits serious consideration. It involves guaranteeing every person an income adequate to meet his or her basic needs. The amount would be lower for children than adults, but would be unaffected by a person's other income, wealth, work, gender, or marital status. It would replace Social Security and existing welfare programs ... If some choose not to work, this should not be considered a problem in a labor-surplus world.

"Such a scheme would be expensive," he acknowledged, "but could be supported in most high-income countries by reducing military spending, corporate welfare, and existing entitlement programs, and increasing taxes on unearned income, luxuries, and user fees on pollution, resource extraction, and other activities a sustainable society needs to discourage."

Such an innovative approach to social engineering, combined with Boshara's Stakeholder concept, would effectively end poverty and "economic" racism, sexism, and ageism, thereby eliminating much of the motivation for crime and social unrest at the bottom of the economic ladder.

But there is a third concept that is even more compelling. Perhaps the most interesting corporate problem-solver alive today is Shann Turnbull, Australian founder of the International Institute for Self-Governance. Although relatively unknown in the U.S., Turnbull's ideas for so-called Ownership Transfer Corporations have greatly excited ethical corporate governance groups and socially responsible investors.

His plan exploits the fact that the attractiveness of most investments is calculated within a relatively short time frame: five to ten years. If investors were given sufficient incentive – a reduction, for example, of corporate taxes from 35 percent to 20 percent – they would agree to transfer five percent of ownership per year to the firm's stakeholder community. Stakeholders are all those who depend upon, are affected by, or add value to a firm, including its customers, employees, suppliers, and local community. If this revolutionary model were followed, all major corporations could be gently dissolved and localized, decentralized, and democratized within a generation. By gradually turning corporations over to those most affected by their decisions, "we the people" would begin to see a new paradigm for democratic corporate responsibility. For more on Turnbull's proposals, see *www.aprim.net/associates/turnbull.htm*.

Based on the comments of Dr. Joseph Hough of Union Theological Seminary, and others, about the responsibility of Christians – and all people of the Abrahamic faiths – in a time of growing crisis, one would hope ideas such as those put forth by Boshara, Korten, and Turnbull would first be embraced from the pulpits of America.

Meanwhile, in his book, *The Theme Is Freedom*, M. Stanton Evans promoted a simple, classically conservative idea that could go a long way toward paying for such redistribution of wealth in a way that could transform American society. "What is needed is ... to establish a particular kind of government: big enough to handle the tasks of keeping order, so that people can go in peace about their business, not so big that it can destroy their freedoms." This "was a problem that defeated the empires, city-states, and philosphers of the pagan era, when authoritarian power always seemed to be the price of order."

With cuts in the bloated and unneccessary defense budget, further cuts in other inappropriately expensive sectors of government, and the elimination of pork-barrel politics, the United States could become a beacon for economic and social reform.

The genesis of such reform, David C. Korten argued in his book, must be the realization, as a people, that "destroying life to make money is a social pathology; democracy is an obvious alternative to corporate rule; a market economy is an obvious alternative to both capitalism and socialism; most people are by nature cooperative and compassionate; human institutions have only the power we choose to yield to them; laws made by people can be changed by people."

In that spirit, despite our present circumstances, it is important to remember another line from Aldous Huxley in *Brave New World*: "Facts don't cease to exist because they are ignored."

If that is the case, perhaps the most important facts that have been ignored for a long time in America were stated by Korten in *When Corporations Rule the World*: "Economic life divorced from spiritual meaning and identity treats life simply as a commodity to be sold to the highest bidder. A civil society, in contrast, rests on a foundation of authentic meaning and purpose."

IX

Becoming an Activist

Chapter 65

A Society Centered on Money or on Life?

Today, "we the people" are working longer and harder for *less* real income, watching the public education system betray the futures of our children, seeing the corporate-owned mass media endlessly repackage institutional lies, and suffering the insult of elected public officials who fail to represent our genuine best interests. We have abandoned a shared hope of taking back our government from corporate special interests and the merciless lobbyists who perpetrate their greed against us daily.

But we are wrong for allowing ourselves to feel that way. Instead of being part of the solution, we are part of the problem. As a nation, as a people, as individual citizens, we must transcend politics and "do the right thing," based on the deep voice of social conscience that has sustained humankind for millennia.

We must remember that one person – a Martin Luther King, Jr., Nelson Mandela, Rosa Parks, Mahatma Gandhi – can make an enormous difference in the world.

In that spirit, we must reach across national and cultural borders and join a growing international phenomenon known as the Living Democracy Movement, cited by David C. Korten in his book as a model for hope and human transformation. Started in India and known as *Jaiv Panchayat* in Hindi, it was co-founded by a woman named Vandana Shiva, a spiritual descendant of Gandhi.

The movement is based on a simple doctrine, stated in The People's Earth Declaration at a UN forum in 1992: "We, the people of the world, will mobilize the forces of transnational civil society behind a widely shared agenda that bonds our many social movements in pursuit of just, sustainable, and participatory human societies. In so doing we are forging our own instruments and processes for redefining the nature and meaning of human progress and for transforming those institutions that no longer respond to our needs."

In its eloquence and power, it is the 21st century international equivalent of the Declaration of Independence. In his book, Korten noted the movement is the political descendant of the Boston Tea Party, which rejected the monopoly power of the prototypical transnational corporation, the British East India Company – owner of the Mayflower and Virginia Land Co. – which wreaked misery not just on the American colonists but every spot on the earth it touched.

In promoting the principles of the movement, Korten quoted Sarah van Gelder, executive editor of *YES!* magazine: "We are working toward a shift from a society centered on the love of money to one centered on the love of life. For me, this simple but powerful idea defines the great work of our time."

In a speech at the World Social Forum in 2002, co-founder Shiva said, "The Living Democracy Movement is simultaneously an ecology movement, an anti-poverty movement … a deepening of democracy movement, a peace movement. It builds on decades of movements defending people's rights to resources; the movements for local, direct democracy; our freedom movements' gifts of Swadeshi [economic sovereignty], Swaraj [self-rule], and Satyagraha [non-cooperation with unjust rule]. It seeks to strengthen rights enshrined in our Constitution ... The most basic right we have as a species is survival, the right to life."

In an open letter to the movement's followers in November 2003, she wrote: "The Living Democracy Movement, which was started on the occasion of World Environment Day on 5th June 1999, at the village Agasthyamuni in the district Rudraprayag, in Garhwal, with 200 villages, has now grown to more than 4,000 villages across the country. Contextually, the movement has grown to include other related issues of land, water, and food."

In an interview with van Gelder in *YES!* magazine in its Summer 2001 issue, David C. Korten said: "Although sometimes characterized by the corporate press as isolationist, it is perhaps the most truly international and inclusive social movement in human history. There is a strong sense of international solidarity and a deep commitment to international cooperation. This is the positive face of globalization – the globalization of civil society. It is a collective human response to the threat posed to the rights and well-being of people everywhere by the globalization of undemocratic institutions."

At a time of growing cynicism and pessimism in the U.S., particularly among young people and the disenfranchised, Korten offered optimism for the world: "It is within our means to make a collective choice for life, though time is fast running out ... The energy for the creative task at hand must flow from a deep love of life and compassion that leads us to reach out to all our neighbors in a joyful anticipation of the world that is ours to create together."

Another organization – U.S.-based – that shares the same basic agenda is the International Forum on Globalization (IFOG), headed by author and economic reformer Jerry Mander. IFOG's board of directors includes Shiva.

"Society is at a crucial crossroads," IFOG noted in a spring 2002 report entitled *A Better World is Possible:*

Alternatives to Economic Globalization. "A peaceful, equitable, and sustainable future depends on the outcome of escalating conflicts between two competing visions: one corporate, one democratic."

In his book, *Unequal Protection*, Thom Hartmann expressed symbolic hope with a chapter entitled, "Restoring the dream of government of the people, by the people, for the people."

In 2004 and beyond, such human inclusion must be, in the spirits of Emma Goldman and Gandhi, among many others, global and anti-nationalist.

Hartmann devoted an entire chapter of his book to Franklin Delano Roosevelt's acceptance speech at the 1936 Democratic Convention, from which he would be re-elected after facing a fascist coup attempt by America's wealthiest and most prominent families two years earlier. "In this world of ours," FDR said, "in other lands, there are some people who, in times past, have lived and fought for freedom, and seem to have grown too weary to carry on the fight. They have sold their heritage of freedom for the illusion of a living. They have yielded their democracy. I believe in my heart that only our success can stir their ancient hope."

He was talking about the fascism that was spreading across Europe, funded and supported by the Bush, Walker, and Harriman families, as well as many other American dynasties, who supported Mussolini and Hitler.

Today, FDR's words can be equally well applied to the American people.

Chapter 66

A 12-Step Program for Changing the World

When a BBC documentary reporter asked Mahatma Gandhi, shortly before his assassination, how he had brought down the British Empire, he noted that he had done nothing of the sort. All he had done, he said, was exert his desire for freedom within his "zone of influence" until all of India realized that it wanted to be free.

In the United States of America of the 21st century, "we the people" are the heirs to a great gift from our Founding Fathers: a heritage of courage and freedom from which even Gandhi took strength. Today, we, too, must invoke it, in the name of all Americans and the people of the world we effectively rule.

"We are now faced with the fury of those who have been deprived for too long of decent lives," American essayist Gore Vidal wrote in a piece entitled "Time for a People's Convention," from his 2002 collection, *The Last Empire: Essays 1992–2000* (Vintage). "It takes no unusual power of prophecy to remark that they will not be apathetic forever ... I submit that we must sit down, and in an orderly way, rethink our entire government, as well as our place in the world."

As one way of accomplishing that, "we the people," as individual citizens and responsible caretakers of the planet, can embrace the emerging creed of the Living Democracy Movement and invoke the memory of Gandhi to work within our "zones of influence" – in our neighborhoods, schools, and workplaces – until all of America wants to be free of corporate rule and white elite domination.

In that spirit, the following is a 12-step program for activism, circulated on the Internet and written by a modern-day patriot named Stanley Campbell. It was sent to me, via e-mail, by a political organizer in Boca Raton, Florida, named Anita Bragin.

"If you have a yearning in your heart to make life better on this planet," Campbell wrote, "to right some wrong or support some effort, large or small, then you are an activist. Instead of feeling frustrated in front of the television set, here are some ways that I've learned to get things done:

1. Speak out about an issue. Don't remain silent, but don't scare people away. Try to express your concern in a positive manner. The world doesn't want you to act, and the rich want you to shop, so God bless the social justice activist! But if you are concerned about the environment, pollution, war, poverty, or the high price of living – or anything else – then speak your mind. Teddy Roosevelt said do what you can, where you are, with what you have.

2. Find like-minded friends. These won't be your real friends – in fact, your real friends will think you are crazy. Pass a petition and sign people up. Folks who give their name and address may give time, energy, and money.

3. Find the official(s) in charge. Everything has got somebody in charge, often a chain of command, and you have to find out to whom to address your concerns. Don't demonize them, for often they are as concerned as you are.

It's not a conspiracy that the world is the way it is. It's just the way it is, and it can be changed.

4. A good organizer keeps track of supporters' names, addresses, telephone numbers, e-mail addresses, and whatever else comes down the pike. Build that list. Share the work, by sharing your concern. Delegation of work means you trust people to help. That trust will help you get things done.

5. Find people who are working on the same issue. And there are always people working on the same issue who've probably won a few battles and can tell you a few stories. It's nice not having to reinvent the wheel.

6. Use resources like libraries and the Internet to educate yourself, and find national organizations that will support you.

7. Bring in speakers, outside agitators, and experts who will enlighten and educate the community as well as the officials. This is a good organizing tool, but don't bust the bank. Find experts who won't demand high fees, but who can share information.

8. Use the media. Make a list of every outlet and try to get personal with the reporters. They are all overworked and appreciate it when someone writes an articulate story for them to use. Don't be afraid of radio talk shows and television cameras. Find spokespeople.

9. Money is no object, but you have to ask for it. Really, this is the richest country in the world, and people will give to a cause if they trust you. So, learn how to beg. Find folks who will keep track of the cash. If you need more than $8,000 a year, find a lawyer and set up a tax-exempt organization, or find an existing group that will take on your cause.

10. Get a copy of *Robert's Rules of Order* and learn its spirit. Your meetings will devolve into squabbles or be driven off track unless you learn how to conduct them. Share responsibilities. To get the book, which city commissions and state legislatures use for efficient meetings, go to *www.robertsrules.com*.

11. Celebrate your victories. Use any excuse to have a party, sing some songs, listen to poetry, and reflect. All the while, charge admission or pass the hat. Try not to treat people on the other side as the enemy.

12. Never say no to somebody else's issue. In fact, encourage people to get up from their television sets and make the world a better place. There are lots of excuses. No one step will bring about redemption, but a whole lot of little steps can get us closer to paradise.

Chapter 67

Mimicking Gandhi:
"Be the Change You Want to See"

T
he important thing to realize in implementing Campbell's call to action is to work on issues that bring us together for the common good rather than those that divide us with partisanship.

The core issue of our time is reclamation of our government, in a common cause characterized by common sense and human decency. Across America, in large cities and small towns, new patriots must be reborn every day from lives of negativity and defeatism. If our children are to have a better life than we have had, it is our responsibility to do all we can to ensure the well-being and survival of the simple, clear values for which the Founding Fathers risked their lives, against all odds – and succeeded.

As a companion set of tactics to Campbell's 12-step program for becoming an activist, consider James Carville's slightly too-partisan 9-step action plan for making the system work, reprinted from his book, *Had Enough?* The same weapons, reprinted here, can be used against errant Democrats, too.

1. Put a member of Congress on the spot. When … members of Congress get generic letters to their offices saying, "Why are you cutting education?" it just rolls off them like water off a duck's back. They believe they can act against their constituents with impunity, and that belief is reinforced by an entire ideological infrastructure that gives them talking points and issue briefs telling them that what they're doing isn't really all that bad. What they're not prepared for is the *specific* critique in their *local* news. So to really put a member of Congress on the spot, send a letter to the editor of your local paper explaining how his or her vote actually hurts your town or state. That'll get to them faster than an oil company lobbyist.

Let me give you one example. A former intern of mine helped put together a series of letters to New Hampshire newspapers asking Congressman John Sununu (now a U.S. Senator) why he was supporting a bill that allowed companies that got Homeland Security government contracts to incorporate offshore to avoid paying taxes. Those letters included mention of specific New Hampshire companies, and guess what: Congressman Sununu changed his vote. Every time a Republican votes against the interests of his or her constituents, they should be similarly embarrassed.

2. Educate yourself. Republicans have built up a cottage industry of books, magazines, policy papers, and other written material that serves to advance their nutty views and specious arguments. That's why you need to arm yourself with facts and counterarguments. There are a lot of places you can do this, but as far as I'm concerned, the progressive must-read is a magazine called *The Washington Monthly*. You can read some of its stuff online and subscribe at *www.washingtonmonthly.com*.

3. Defend your ideas. You've just read a book full of ideas … you've got strongly held views. Don't keep 'em to yourself. Don't cede arguments with knuckleheads at cocktail parties and barbecues. You've got the tools: take 'em to task.

4. Volunteer support for a public servant. A lot of good public servants labor in obscurity - and a lot of bad ones give the good ones a bad name. If you see someone serving honorably, that's someone worth supporting with your time and energy.

5. Participate. Call or write your Congressperson, go to a town hall or school board meeting ... the vocal majority beats the silent majority every day of the week and twice on Sundays.

6. Write a check. I hate to say it, but money talks. The least we can do is make it say the right things. Sit down, figure out what causes or candidates are important to you and how much you can afford to give, and write a check.

7. Vote, and make sure a like-minded friend does, too. I bet you didn't know that we have a way to have a national "recall" election – it's called an *election*. If you didn't vote, and didn't make your like-minded friends vote, you have no right to come whining to me.

8. Aggravate a Republican. Every time I see a car with a BUSH-CHENEY sticker, one of my favorite things to do is pull up alongside them, motion for them to roll down the window, and when they do, I say, "Hey, I just thought you should know – somebody put a BUSH-CHENEY sticker on your car." This doesn't really help anything, but you'll find it very therapeutic.

9. Be positive. Don't just let people know when they're doing bad, let 'em know when they're doing good. Like I said in the beginning: We need more of [a get-it-done] attitude and less of the cynical negativity that dominates so much political discussion today.

If you want to go even further than Campbell and Carville suggest and become a full-fledged citizen-lobbyist, an excellent informational resource, to be combined with the tactics listed by the two writers, is the *U.S. Congress Handbook*, published by Votenet Solutions, Inc. in Washington, D.C. It lists every member of the U.S. House of Representatives and the Senate, as well as their key staff members, from chief of staff to scheduler. It also lists the memberships and top staff members of each of the major committees of the two houses of Congress, and contact information for key federal government agencies and other political resources. For good measure, it also includes the Declaration of Independence, the Constitution, and the Bill of Rights, and explains the powers of Congress, how a bill becomes a law, and how the Electoral College works. It can be ordered online at *www.uscongresshandbook.com*.

"With your help, we can and will change the winds blowing in this nation," anti-Dominionist journalist Katherine Yurica has written at her web site. "Liberty and freedom belong to all Americans, not just to a selected elite. Rush Limbaugh and his ilk have spread poison all over America. It's a worse poison than anthrax or nerve gas. Those poisons will only kill our bodies, but the poison of the right wing talk show hosts and the religious right can and does enslave the souls of a free people and destroys all that is good and pure and noble in this land."

In order to defend all that is good, pure, and noble – in America and the world at large – remember always the words of Gandhi, as invoked in a consultation on this book by Vermont human rights activist John Wilmerding: "You must be the change you wish to see in the world ... Use truth as your anvil, nonviolence as your hammer, and anything that does not stand the test when it is brought to the anvil of truth, reject it ... Recall the face of the poorest and most helpless person you have ever seen, and ask yourself if the next worldly action that you contemplate is going to be of any use to that person."

Most important, perhaps, in the context of America's ferocious nationalism of 2004, resulting in beheadings by Muslim insurgents and the prison torture by U.S. troops at Abu Ghraib in Iraq, remember the words that came to be known in the 1950s as the Nuremberg Principle: "Individuals have global moral obligations which transcend national obligations of obedience; they must sometimes violate domestic laws to prevent crimes against peace, justice, and all of humanity."

For inspiration – belief that *you* can make a difference, right now – remember the words of the late Robert F. Kennedy: "It is from numberless diverse acts of courage and belief that human history is shaped. Each time a man stands up for an ideal, or acts to improve the lot of others, or strikes out against injustice, he sends forth a tiny ripple of hope, and crossing each other from a million different centers of energy and daring, these ripples build a current that can sweep down the mightiest walls of oppression and resistance."

And finally, given the tenor of our times, remember the words of Benjamin Franklin upon the signing of the Declaration of Independence: "We must all hang together, or assuredly we shall all hang separately."

In the spirit of the Living Democracy Movement, in the names of peace and freedom, remember the words of Thomas Paine, from *Common Sense* in the fateful year 1776: "We have it in our power to begin the world over again."

INDEX